The Financial Protector

CHRISTOPHER A. MURRAY
MURRAY FINANCIAL GROUP

Christopher A. Murray/Murray Financial Group

50 Carroll Creek Way, Suite 240

Frederick, Maryland 21701

https://murrayfinancialgroup.com/

The Financial Protector/Christopher A. Murray. —1st ed.

ISBN 9798711099710

The contents of this book are provided for informational purposes only and are not intended to serve as the basis for any financial decisions. Any tax, legal, or estate planning information is general in nature. It should not be construed as legal or tax advice. Always consult an attorney or tax professional regarding the applicability of this information to your unique situation.

The content of this book should not be construed as personalized investment advice nor should it be interpreted as an offer to buy or sell any securities mentioned. A financial advisor should be consulted before implementing any of the strategies presented.

Investing involves risk, including the potential loss of principal. No investment strategy can guarantee a profit or protect against loss in periods of declining values. Any references to protection benefits or guaranteed/lifetime income streams refer only to fixed insurance products, not securities or investment products. Insurance and annuity product guarantees are backed by the financial strength and claims-paying ability of the issuing insurance company.

We do not provide tax or legal advice. You are expressly advised to consult with a qualified attorney or tax professional to determine your legal or tax needs.

Investment advisory services offered through Murray Financial Group, Inc., a Registered Investment Adviser.

GOD IS GOOD, PRAISE HIM.

"The only wealth in this world is children."
— Michael Corleone, Godfather III

Table of Contents

Christopher Murray

Preface

Farm work rarely factored into our family lifestyle when I was a kid.

Never did I imagine at this point in my life I would have the opportunity to feed animals, muck stalls, or halter break . . . let alone live on a twenty-one-acre homestead where we taught our own kids such chores and invite 4-H participants to learn the tasks necessary to show dairy heifers at the county fair.

My two older brothers, Steve and Dave, as well as myself, learned the value of hard work and perseverance from our mother, who raised us on her own.

Steve and Dave actually worked on an uncle's dairy farm when I was just a toddler, but I mostly stayed near the house and helped in the garden. I only got out in the fields while riding in a truck alongside my grandfather when he delivered sandwiches to everyone for lunch.

Nonetheless, occasional farm work as a toddler didn't shape me into someone familiar with the many details of farming. That made me no different than a lot of my classmates. We attended schools in rural areas of Howard County, where the population totaled 287,085 in the 2010 census. Characteristics, however, regarding most residents could be linked to the urban sprawl of those working in nearby Baltimore and Washington, D.C.

When a high school buddy asked if I was interested in working on a dairy farm for a little summer money going into my senior year of high school, I could easily have declined, thinking it wasn't something that interested me.

But I didn't think twice. The chance to work with friends and enjoy the outdoors was a perfect match.

Turns out, that seemingly trivial nod of the head on where to work my last summer as a high school student may have been the best decision I ever made. I doubt I would have met, or at least I would not have ever dated, my wife, Carole.

The dairy farm I worked on belonged to Carole's family. Both our relationship, and the farm work I wholeheartedly embraced, changed my life. That became obvious even as we both walked the hallways of Glenelg High School in Howard County.

That senior year I spoke with a recruiter and considered joining the military. But I knew Carole, who was a junior that year, intended to pursue her interest in business education by enrolling at Towson University. I knew we probably wouldn't stay together if I enlisted, and we would become separated on different continents. So, I declined.

Was I love struck? No doubt. My wife and I enjoy a relationship that benefits from adoring intuition. Like the day Carole was holding our first child, Devin, and noticed her maternity leave dwindling down to precious time left spending her entire day with our newborn son.

Out of the blue, she began bawling.

"What is going on?" I asked.

"I don't want to leave him," Carole said.

Precisely what I wanted to hear. It could be I offered my approval far too casually, as if I was asking Carole what we were going to do for dinner.

But I wanted her to volunteer any desire to stay at home with Devin. I did not want to raise the possibility myself because any impulse, any deliberation, and any decision first required she think it through herself.

Her marketing career for an insurance company had blossomed from hours of dedication and sacrifice earning her degree from Towson, so I knew it wouldn't be an easy choice.

I wanted her to fully support, and even propose, the switch to stay-at-home mom. Then, I wasted no time endorsing the idea she "brought up." Of course, I also realized our source for family income had just shifted. Sole responsibility rested with me as we would eventually raise three wonderful children—our sons, Devin and Garrett, and our daughter, Morgan.

****

Pressure is a privilege.

I cannot recall when I first heard the saying or sensed it rolling through my brain.

It could have been on the motocross starting line alongside a full gate of forty riders charging into the first corner, wide open.

Then again, I might have discovered pressure is a privilege after moving out of the first home Carole and I bought to take on the responsibilities presented by our twenty-one-acre farmstead in Howard County. That place has provided our family the space we need to live out our dreams. In fact, before any construction began, Carole and the kids came up with the perfect name for our new home and the land it sits on, "Abundant Blessings."

No question, the decision I made to create my own sandbox in the financial services industry contained its share of worries and trepidation that often factor into pressure.

But only if I let it.

Landscaping gave me my start in business. Although I acquired jobs from high-end builders, my lack of resources prohibited my start-up from taking on bigger, more lucrative, projects.

A developer from whom I purchased farm supplies agreed to buy my business and bought the machinery needed to bid on bigger jobs. Yet, I grew antsy because I saw this same person succeed in other pursuits such as real estate. I wanted something similar for myself.

Attempts through him to expand my business interests stalled, so I turned to another avenue—the newspaper want-ads. New York Life Securities was looking for anyone eager to sell, and, after getting through that door and into the financial industry, I later moved to Principal Financial.

For both of those big-box companies I sold proprietary products. That grows tiring. We tend to settle on favorite brands sometimes when we shop, particularly with cars and colas. But we also like to be able to shop from a variety of options for various goods, something I was unable to provide until becoming an independent wealth and retirement advisor.

A group of us split away from Principal Financial and opened a shop in Columbia, Maryland. Eventually, I started my own firm, Murray Financial Group, in 1995 and worked ever since to build that practice in Frederick, Maryland. We have clients from all over the country.

Pressure? I guess. Knowing any mistakes are all on me can be a vulnerable feeling, not to mention lonesome. On most occasions, however, adrenaline conquers fright. I stay focused on doing the right thing and realize my own practice is the best space for me.

Prayer plays a powerful role, too, in all matters. Our faith in God's plan convinced Carole and I that all the significant developments in our marriage—a single income, a growing family, a new house, additional land, and farm expenses—made perfect sense.

I knew, too, that I wanted to make a difference in people's lives by helping them make the most out of the hard-earned dollars they invested.

Also, when I began wearing sleeves after leaving my landscaping business to join the financial industry, the spray starch I learned to use allowed me to dress the part. Many times, I found myself alongside those whose privileges didn't come from pressure but rather resources given to them by their parents. And yet, I knew my upbringing, especially the values gained through hard work, gave me an advantage.

****

Credit my mother, and the starch she poured into a comment I'll never forget, for helping me present myself in the right way.

One Saturday night, all of thirteen years old, I wanted to go out with friends but couldn't find a pair of clean jeans. So, I approached my mother and, with the direct tone I maintain to this day, asked about an unattended pile of dirty clothes. Specifically, the jeans I wanted washed.

She glared at me and said, quite simply, "If you want your clothes washed, then wash them yourself." That moment remains one of my most memorable exchanges with my mother, a strong woman who drove each day from our rural home in Howard County into Baltimore where she worked for a large real estate company.

Not only did I need to wash my jeans, I also needed directions for how to do laundry. Shamefully looking at my shoelaces after realizing she was right and I was wrong for assuming she was solely responsible for washing clothes, I proceeded to ask about detergent measurements, washer temperatures, and dryer settings.

I don't know why that exchange still stands out. But it does make me chuckle a bit understanding now that it was her way of helping me become self-sufficient.

To this day, Mom gets along wonderfully, is active in the community, and visits our home at least a couple of times a week.

After retiring once, my Mom returned to work part-time for the same real estate company, driving into downtown Baltimore from her rural home in Howard County. For years she was a rental agent manager for the properties the company rents. I learned from her how to present myself as professionally as possible and how to handle trying conversations with patience and class.

I credit not only my mother for raising me right, even through lean times, but also my oldest brother, Steve.

We started racing motocross together when Steve was nineteen and I was twelve. Steve took a genuine interest in everything I did and was a great influence. Later down the road, we were neighbors with Steve and his family when we both bought 3-acre tracts.

Now we live close to Carole's parents, who also carry a huge influence. So much so that Carole and I continued the leasing program Dave and Ann started, which enables local kids to work chores at "Abundant Blessings" in preparation for showing dairy heifers part of the year.

Necessities involved with life on the farm find Carole and I out doing chores in the morning and evening. Her folks, who live just down the road, continue daily farm chores well before dawn every day as they enter their nineties.

Family is vital to me. I emphasize family values as a fundamental component to my advisory practice. I truly enjoy listening to clients share their cherished memories and principled desires involving their loved ones while realizing I am truly blessed and grateful for everyone I call family.

'Your Financial Editor'

T he advantages of my regular appearances on radio are noticeable practically every time someone steps into my office. Usually, they already know me. Well, they at least recognize my voice and whatever images are conveyed by the dialogue I share on WFMD-AM (930) radio in Frederick.

Often, I find an inherent trust is formed because of the business news updates I do three times each weekday morning and on my hour-long show, Your Financial Editor, which airs on Saturday.

Radio is described as "theater of the mind," and it is my intent to leave a friendly and personable impression anytime I'm on the air, while also sharing my views on financial matters.

I have spent more than twenty years providing daily business updates and wrapping up with in-depth analyses during my weekend show. Half of that hour on Saturday is spent providing perspective on the week's news, and the other half is a thirty-minute interview with a select guest or a deeper look at a trending topic.

I certainly sense that the Frederick market recognizes me as a reliable source of information to help them gain insight into the complex world of finance. The impact from those radio appearances also reaches into the sizeable Washington and Baltimore markets, as well as other communities in Maryland, Pennsylvania, and Virginia.

Existing clients often remember something I mentioned on the air. Sometimes the subject matter prompts them to think about their own portfolio and ideas they want to kick around.

Because prospective clients feel as if they know me already, it loosens the restraints on what can sometimes be a rigid first conversation regarding finances and retirement ambitions.

Many who embark on the process of finding a financial advisor are unaccustomed to such dialogue and want to spare themselves any embarrassment they think may arise from past decisions they made on their own.

Believe me, anything to lighten their burden and make them more comfortable engaging in the important financial discussion they know is necessary can be a relief. You don't need to cultivate a certain warmth or comfort level, because it's already established. For me, radio is an icebreaker for getting that first conversation to flow smoothly.

I lucked out, though. Not long after starting my own practice in Frederick, a buddy of mine introduced me to a woman he was dating. She worked as a sales rep for WFMD and asked me what I did to promote my business.

At the time, I did virtually nothing. As a new start-up, I needed to cover office costs and carefully adhere to a tight budget in order to get my firm off the ground.

To sell me on some radio advertising, the salesperson structured a year-long strategy for commercial time. I agreed to the proposal, as much as anything as a favor to my buddy and his girlfriend.

After we got started down that path, though, I got to wondering about getting involved in helping the station with actual news content. It made sense to me, even though I had no background in radio, because the station thrived on its "talk" format and could add yet another dimension with business programming.

A conversation with the WFMD program director, Frank Mitchell, got me in the game, and I've been in the lineup ever since. The AM station features nationally syndicated segments each weekday from Glenn Beck, Rush Limbaugh, and Sean Hannity.

I do my updates with "The Morning Mayor," Bob Miller, a local personality I am proud to call my friend. Each day we exchange friendly banter when I do my updates. His show, The Morning News Express, keeps chugging away after all these years, informing faithful listeners in Frederick and beyond.

My show never interrupted that array of heavy hitters since it helped fill the station's weekend schedule. In addition to their AM dial, listeners can hear my show digitally by tuning in on WFMD's website. Your Financial Editor is also available on podcasts through iTunes.

The hour-long program I first tried to do centered on a specific financial topic. Realize that I had no training and no coaching in radio. I winged it on my own.

Although I made it through those shows without throwing up, my stomach churned, and it was a wonder I didn't get sick. The pressure to fill time by chatting on and on about specific financial elements could be grueling and downright repetitive.

It's partly why I've never conducted many of the dinner seminars so many financial advisors rely on for prospecting clients. Doing the same presentation over and over becomes monotonous. And, if the presenter is bored, just think about those in the audience, many of whom responded to a mailer so they could eat a free steak. As a financial advisor, I can find better ways to spend my time and money.

When my hour of radio time seemed to be dragging along, I changed it up and devoted the first thirty minutes to recapping the week. To do this, I stay abreast of the news, especially in the financial sector. I thought that time spent recapping the week's activities could provide insight into pressing developments people missed during the hustle and bustle of their work week.

Yet, I still had thirty minutes to fill. The idea to separate that portion of my show into something different seemed appealing, especially if it could be filled with informative guests.

Once I unveiled that format, some persistent people I didn't even know proved eager to help me out.

One thing about radio is, once you become established or even noticed, public relations firms contact you to book guests. Being close to Washington D.C., engaging personalities are plentiful.

A memorable breakthrough for Your Financial Editor came when I booked Louis Rukeyser, a longtime television host who became renowned in financial circles for his weekly show, Wall $treet Week.

That program sometimes triggered Monday spikes in stock prices for a company touted by Rukeyser during the analysis he offered on Fridays. Rukeyser agreed to be on my show a couple of times. He always had something of his own to promote, but that was fine because of the credible information he dispensed.

Since those early days, guests have come from diverse backgrounds, and the conversations are interesting to hear, flow quite naturally, and are fun for me to steer along.

At one point in the late 1990s, I got into communications with representatives for Donald Trump. Obviously, this was long before his triumphant surge to the presidency in the 2016 election. So long ago, in fact, that communications went through a fax machine.

By my estimation, chances grew to about 80 percent that Trump would appear on my show based on the tone of the communications with his office. A different person on his end became involved, however, and we didn't get Trump booked.

Nonetheless, my guests have included Federal Reserve officials, corporate CEOs, entrepreneurs, moguls, professors, economists, ambassadors, historians, and journalists. Among them:

- **Sheila C. Bair**, former chairperson of the U.S. Federal Deposit Insurance Corporation
- **The Hon. Kim Beazley**, AC, former Australian Ambassador to the U.S.

- **Liz Claman**, Emmy Award-winning anchor of Countdown to the Closing Bell on FOX Business Network
- **Douglas Feith**, former Undersecretary of Defense for Policy; director of Hudson's Center for National Security Strategies
- **Louis Ferrante**, crime and business writer and host of Inside the Gangster's Code on Discovery Channel; former Gambino family mobster
- **Melissa Francis**, anchor on FOX Business Network
- **Daniel Hannan**, former Member of the European Parliament; British journalist, author, and politician
- **Karen Kerrigan**, President and CEO of the Small Business & Entrepreneurship Council
- **Jeffrey Lacker**, former president of the Federal Reserve Bank of Richmond
- **Sebastian Mallaby**, senior fellow for international economics at the Council on Foreign Relations; journalist and author
- **Wilfred M. McClay**, Blankenship Chair in the History of Liberty, University of Oklahoma; educator, author
- **The Hon. Christos P. Panagopoulos**, Greek Ambassador to the U.S.
- **Harvey Rosenblum**, former Executive Vice President and Director of Research at the Federal Reserve Bank of Dallas
- **The Hon. Manuel Sager**, Swiss Ambassador to the U.S.
- **Amity Shlaes**, Bloomberg View columnist; director of the Four Percent Growth Project at the George W. Bush Institute
- **Diane Swonk**, Chief Economist at Grant Thornton
- **Jonathan Tisch**, Chairman and CEO of Loews Hotels

We aired my first one-hour program live at 6 p.m. on a Saturday night. I will never forget that day, but not for the reason you might imagine (considering I was making my radio debut). Earlier that day at a political fundraiser, I met Oliver North, the retired Marine Corps lieutenant colonel. We spoke for a couple of minutes, and later he appeared on my show a couple of times. He never wanted anything for his appearance. He'd just come on the show, share his stories, and be gracious with his time. Meeting him has truly been one of the greatest highlights of my show.

My show is conservative by nature. That approach aligns with advice I offer investors with their decisions and retirees with the plans they trust me to build. Politically, I roll the same way without getting in your face about my conservative beliefs.

Fortunately, I learned to be choosy in booking guests. Those I don't agree with morally, or whose viewpoints I don't accept, I don't invite. There's no point in getting combative while interviewing anyone or drifting into territory that doesn't align with my values.

That way, I can confidently make the final half-hour of Your Financial Editor about the guest. The credibility successful people bring to the show is also a reflection on my practice. On occasion, financial analysis or practical sense they espouse can be incorporated into investment and retirement recommendations I pass on to my clients. I learn something from every interview I conduct, and the information helps create a deeper understanding of issues we face.

Again, I am truly grateful for the opportunities provided by WFMD and the friendships I forged with Frank Mitchell, the program director, and Bob Miller, the morning show host. Each has been with the station as long as I've been doing my thing. Each helped greatly with calming my nerves and growing comfortable with all I do. Also, they go to bat for me anytime ownership of the station changes.

Frank and Bob have been adamant about the value I bring. Believe me, it takes time to develop authentic rapport with a host. The exchanges with Bob during my hourly updates each weekday morning at 5:50, 6:50, and 7:50 are like two buddies talking over coffee.

I do the updates from home, where often I happen to also be engaged in morning chores. That can lead to some unusual circumstances listeners cannot detect . . . unless our chocolate Labrador happens to bark, and I tell radioland my "intern analyst" is acting up.

One morning between the 6:50 and 7:50 a.m. updates, our two horses got out. Running through our neighbors' soybean field, I thought my heart would explode chasing them down. I finally got them settled and led one down the road to our farmstead while the other followed. My wife, Carole ,trailed them in our car with the blinkers flashing.

The scene looked like something out of The Beverley Hillbillies. Then, unexpectedly, the alarm went off on my phone. Time for me to do a radio update. So, I called in to the station. Once I got on the air, I just knew a horse would whinny or, possibly, even act up. But the horses remained calm. I walked them into their pasture, and no listener ever knew of my morning calamity as I gave the update without any notes.

The banter I share with Bob makes my day. I send him an email each morning about issues I'll touch on in the earliest segment, then I analyze the markets and provide information in each update about high points people should monitor that day in the financial sector.

Zingers are something Bob throws out from time to time to offer me a chance to run with something that reflects my conservative leanings without being too obstinate.

For example, during the third year of Donald Trump's presidency, with his re-election bid beginning to take shape, I disputed numerous reports that warned of a possible recession.

The country had been through the longest period of uninterrupted gains in American history, so analysts lined up to predict an end to the bull market because, well, that's what happens . . . markets do experience corrections. At some point, it made sense someone would time their prediction to coincide with an actual market downturn.

As it turned out, the country did slide into a recession after the adverse effects of the coronavirus contributed to twenty-two million Americans losing their jobs. Despite steep declines in the market, many analysts predicted the recession would be one of the shortest on record.

Keep in mind, it took a catastrophic world-wide pandemic to tank the U.S. economy. It could be that it satisfied some analysts and politicians who seemed to almost be rooting for such financial carnage.

"People are trying to talk this economy into a recession," I cautioned listeners prior to the threat posed by COVID-19.

With the tone I apply to any conversation, I added my take on the motivation behind some of the analysts' predictions.

"Some people go as far as to say they want a recession so the administration will be gone," I said.

I proceeded to pick apart the selfishness exhibited in that kind of mindset. Recessions cause people to lose jobs. If that happens, they could lose their cars, or, worse yet, their houses. A financial crisis can even rip apart families. During the Great Recession from 2007 to 2009, suicide rates rose sharply in the United States.

"So, for someone to come out and say that they want a recession— think about the evil in that," I told listeners.

Radio gives me a platform to be me. Since it also provides a platform to promote my business, I tend to believe I cater to clients who are like-minded, which suits me perfectly.

I'm not afraid to get out there, call people out, and tell the audience what I think. I don't get wrapped up in talking colors, such as red or blue. I just say what I want to say. It works out fine for me, based on the business radio has generated, and it seems to work for WFMD, based on my regular appearances with the station.

Chapter One

The Fresh Approach

O kay, so I'm on radio three times a day, five times a week. Sounds as if I can really babble on, right? Well, I like to think I do a good job finding material for the financial updates I provide 930 WFMD.

Also, the hour-long show I conduct on Saturdays includes my own delivery on a variety of business developments that happened during the week. Then, I typically interview a special guest.

So, yes, I suppose you can assume I recognized my gift for gab and tied it up in a bow and ribbon for my program, *Your Financial Editor*.

In my practice as a financial wealth and retirement planner, however, I take the most pride in being a good listener. In particular, the initial consultation I engage in with potential clients is designed for me to recognize and appreciate the journey that led to their desire to plan for retirement. As the conversation unfolds, I find great joy in learning their retirement vision.

Each time I meet clients for the first time, a new story unfolds. This helps keep what I do, well, "fresh," for the listeners and myself.

Chances are good that anyone who arranges an appointment has already heard my voice at some point on the radio or received a reference from one of our other clients. If they listened to me on the air, what they heard hopefully built a modest degree of trust in me before they ever walked into my office.

So, it's easy for me to stay relatively quiet and find out what convinced them it was time to consult with a financial advisor about a retirement plan. Sometimes I will ask why they phrased their observation the way they did.

"You answered this question a certain way on the radio, and I got a sense for how you might work with me," they'll tell me.

That can be quite humbling. Nonetheless, I insist clients be themselves. After all, this is their retirement, built upon their hard-earned money. They know, deep down, how they want to enjoy what is a new journey in life. If not, they need to begin thinking in those terms.

Questions are certainly in order. Lots of them, hopefully. I strive to build trust—both with those who listen to me every weekday and those I listen to when they come to my office seeking financial advice.

How they embark on their retirement journey is something we hope potential clients view as a "fresh approach," part of the seven-step retirement strategy Murray Financial Group trademarked in the early 2000s as The Financial Protector™ process.

The steps we outline allow people to monitor what we are doing while we continually provide explanation. We believe this to be an act of transparency. That's a word that too often gets thrown around nearby in Washington politics without a great deal of actual commitment.

Sometimes it takes a considerable leap of faith for people to meet with a wealth and retirement advisor. It could be they mistrusted a previous financial professional. Or, they simply want a second opinion, as financial strategies change when approaching retirement. Or, they simply have never sought advice about finances, sometimes because they did not want to admit their lack of knowledge or interest.

Whatever their experiences, I want prospective clients to get their feelings and their thoughts into the open. I promise to politely listen. I will also answer all questions and concerns honestly, with no nonsense.

Planning is Powerful

Imagine the materials for your dream home are dumped at the five-acre lot you recently purchased because of its wonderful view.

The lumber and drywall to build the walls, the cement needed to pour the foundation, the shingles for the roof, the beautiful tile that will accent your other flooring, the richly textured cabinets, and even the tub enclosures are spread throughout your property. It seems like everything, including the literal kitchen sink, is strewn everywhere.

No blueprint, however, can be found. You're left to figure out everything on your own. That hammer you hope to swing begins to look pretty small, doesn't it?

Obviously, you need a plan to make all the materials fit the correct measurements and angles.

You realize this. You've planned things before. For example, vacations. You examined routes to the extent you even knew what highways were under construction. You made sure to find hotels where fares were reduced because of reward points you accrued and looked for where the locals eat, gladly breaking the chain for a meal or two.

So why, particularly when vacations are often planned so meticulously, is retirement planning overlooked by far too many Americans? Retirement is more than some occasional event. It encompasses every waking minute once you voluntarily leave the full-time workforce for good and rely on your life savings for income.

Frankly, retirement should be the most wonderful time of your life. A chance, perhaps, to travel for an extended period. Time to attend grandkids' activities. You may handle a hot glue gun or hot putter (if the golf gods cooperate) as you either rediscover old hobbies or take up new ones.

Wouldn't it be nice to know how far your retirement savings will go and how to make them last? Especially if proper planning can help you do the things you never quite enjoyed to the fullest during your work career?

Guessing how much income you will need . . . not knowing whether you will be a burden on your children . . . hoping things will be okay . . . these are not concerns you should carry throughout retirement. Believe me, I do not toss a dart, roll the dice, or flip a coin when crafting your retirement plan.

I do, however, commend anyone who arranges a visit to Murray Financial Group for the complimentary initial consultation we conduct in our Frederick office.

While the act of scheduling an appointment is relatively painless, we know stepping in front of a financial planner can be unnerving. It could be you're seeking a second opinion after wondering if a current financial advisor or broker is still a good fit.

Or, it could be you have never made such an appointment before with a financial specialist. In such cases, trepidation can mount over time. Some are reluctant to seek professional financial advice for whatever reason. Often, we see people who feel in over their heads. Well, if so, that is the best reason of all for a specialist to look at your portfolio and begin the planning process.

The accumulation of assets can almost seem like an automated process once you learn to appreciate the concept of saving for retirement. You set aside an amount from each paycheck, let retirement accounts build, and watch them grow. Smart investors even schedule increases to their retirement contributions, which are timed to coincide with periodic raises.

When you retire, however, a completely different mindset and approach is required to prevent you from outliving the income you will need. This transition will find you confronting several variables related to the five pillars of retirement—income, investments, taxes, legacy, and health care. The need to preserve your wealth makes it critical you work with a qualified wealth and retirement advisor.

If the best time for you to consult with an advisor about retirement was years ago, then the second-best time is now.

Adjusting with Circumstances

Rick and Joyce waited to seek out a financial planner, though the relatively simple investments in their portfolio grew appreciably over the years. A rosy outlook was beginning to emerge when they were in their late fifties and scheduled their first visit with me.

Although many of my clients call me after seeing other advisors, Rick and Joyce managed their affairs and their accounts themselves before coming to see me. They finally relented to seeing an advisor after realizing, responsibly, the many variables in retirement. Planning for all of them, and understanding how those variables intertwine, can be tricky.

In the case of Rick and Joyce, a retirement cottage on the Delaware shore was their delightful reward for a life spent raising a fine family with unconditional love and support. The shore offered a beautiful place for grandkids to visit. They sensed this was an attainable goal after their devotion to building an impressive sum in their 401(k) accounts to provide the foundation for a secure retirement.

Unfortunately, trouble arose shortly after we began to chart a course for when to retire. We were just beginning to draft a plan when Rick called to inform us his circumstances had changed. His company phased out his lucrative engineering job; Rick was let go.

The best possible solution arose from his first impulse—find another position that paid a comparable salary. Joyce also continued to work, though her position as an office assistant paid less than the job Rick held for many years.

The search for a comparable salary proved difficult for Rick, a situation that is relatively commonplace, according to a *ProPublica* analysis of American workers age fifty and above. Fifty-six percent of older workers who engaged in the *ProPublica* study were laid off at least once. Of those workers, one in ten earned as much as they did before their termination.[1]

Those are gloomy numbers, which we have seen transpire on occasion with some of our clients—particularly those working at companies that have changed ownership and downsized. Also, new business models and concepts can, unfortunately, create new job requirements and expectations that jeopardize roles previously established for long-time employees.

After we crunched the numbers for Rick and Joyce, we determined they could retire to the Delaware shore, though it required them to sell their existing home sooner than they anticipated. Also, they needed to adhere to a tighter budget. That was not a hardship for them, largely because they did so well throughout their careers of saving into retirement accounts and budgeting wisely.

They came to our office wondering if and when retirement was a possibility. Just like them, I like to tell clients that the planning process we initiate will incorporate some math and some science while producing a comprehensive, yet practical, plan to follow in retirement. The concern Rick and Joyce rightfully acknowledged regarding an income shortage after Rick was laid off proved to be an alteration we could incorporate into their plan.

Few Surprises in This Business

Nothing, it seems, truly surprises me.

It could be because I look for the facts, providing daily business updates at 5:50, 6:50, and 7:50 each morning. Time spent finding nuggets for those segments and then pointing out aspects that often go

---

[1] Peter Gosselin. ProPublica. Dec. 28, 2018. "If You're Over 50, Chances Are the Decision to Leave a Job Won't be Yours." https://www.propublica.org/article/older-workers-united-states-pushed-out-of-work-forced-retirement

undetected and unreported often allows me to unearth more "Man Bites Dog" stories than some can imagine. Remember, too, that the political discourse in Washington often generates its share of surreal storylines and sub-plots.

So again, little surprises me.

Many clients I work with as a planner are learned people. Whatever their areas of expertise, they are often armed with a college degree and, in many cases, postgraduate degrees.

I would be remiss, however, not to acknowledge the many blue- and grey-collar workers I can proudly point to as clients.

I feel in my role as a financial planner as though I administer an exam before someone arrives for an initial visit. We pose several questions for potential clients to answer during our onboarding process. We also ask that they bring a will or trust, if they have them to the first meeting. Finally, we want them to bring account statements from bank accounts, money markets, CDs, any investment accounts, and any retirement accounts.

Typically, all their stuff is stacked into a tidy pile right next to where they are sitting. Yet, I do not look at it immediately after our introductions. During the first meeting, which is complimentary and free of commitment, I want everyone, including myself, to determine whether I can provide something of value to someone's situation.

On occasion, it becomes obvious I can't.

I am certain all wealth and retirement advisors, to some degree, run across potential clients who feel as if they are the smartest in the room.

I remember a couple, each of whom was approaching their mid-fifties, walking into my office. The wife was neatly dressed and quite courteous. From the outset it became apparent she didn't make many financial decisions. Any number that could follow a dollar sign seemingly received the sole consideration of her husband.

Shortly after we said our hellos, he launched into a cursory overview of the financial markets, the federal reserve, and trade talks. I politely listened as he eventually attempted to touch on what he considered the entirety of the planning process. He acknowledged that he had been managing this, that, and the other through his brokerage account.

I'm not sure I ever fielded a question, but I knew how a relationship would probably go with this couple. I honestly did not think I could make an impact.

After listening politely for the better part of a half-hour, I asked, "Well, is there anything else I can answer for you?"

I noticed my question puzzled the couple—the man because he was intent to prove he knew everything about finance; the woman because as disengaged as she was, she knew I hadn't gotten a word in edgewise, least of all in the form of a question.

Imagine their surprise when I politely ended the meeting.

"I think you are doing a great job," I told them. "From everything you explained to me, you follow the markets closely, you understand what is going on with the GDP in China, and it seems as if you've done really, really well with your investments. I don't think I can do any better. I think you should probably keep doing what you are doing."

While that response often floors people, and did to this couple to some extent, the man quickly regained his swagger and told his wife, "See, honey, I told you we were all good."

It could be he is smarter than me, and I'm fine with that. I wished them well as they left and truly meant it. But if I prepared a financial retirement plan for them, it was obvious they'd never be happy. Before long he'd be calling to ask when to invest in Stock A or Stock B because he'd been charting those investments, and others. The insight he'd want would be outside the scope of the hardcore retirement planning I provide.

For clients I do take on who remain intent on playing the market, I suggest setting up a "fun money" account I'm not going to be associated with. That way, if the latest cryptocurrency falls to zero, the decision to invest was all on them. If that happens, clients are accountable for their actions, and they usually start re-thinking the idea of a separate investment, especially if the "fun" is removed from their money.

Family Matters

You know what bothered me most about the couple I determined needed no assistance from me? It wasn't the overbearing nature of the "financial genius." No, even more troubling was I never grasped any obvious commitment to family.

Oh, the couple did have children. It said so on one of the first pages of the onboarding questionnaire they filled out before their first meeting.

Yet, they never mentioned their kids. I guess I could have calculated their ages to know what benchmarks these parents witnessed, but I heard nothing about high school activities, a church confirmation, or college pursuits. Nothing to enlighten me about weddings or careers, hardships or milestones. Nothing trivial, either, despite all the years that pass between diaper changes and driver's ed.

Nothing.

That's a red flag for me when I meet with someone for the first time. My background, I think, enables me to empathize with clients and potential clients. In addition, it allows me to be a pretty good judge of character.

Please note how I categorize those who make appointments and engage in "The Fresh Approach." I call them *potential* clients.

Not everyone will find me to be the wealth and retirement advisor they want to consult. This is fine. Quite frankly, it's wise to sit down and kick the tires with multiple advisors when planning for your retirement. Again, this is your life and your money. Clients who visit with me last often comment that I am capable of explaining, and simplifying, what it is they were told by others.

I am a family man who married his high school sweetheart. We raised three kids. Values related to family are precious for us and a character trait I look for in everyone.

Call me old school if you want. But to me, the construct of the fiduciary standard already requires me, as a registered investment advisor, to act solely in my client's best interest. I've been doing this since 1995. As the fiduciary standard has gained notoriety, and, indeed, popularity, since then, I tell clients they can link me to the song lyric, "I was country when country wasn't cool."

Still, I have difficulty determining the best interest of a client if they have essentially turned their backs on family. Something within such a relationship has turned so fundamentally wrong that I can't, in good faith, work for such clients. Unless, of course, a satisfactory reason exists causing strained relations within the family, it's often the case their values simply are not aligned with mine.

We're put here for a reason, and I believe it's to make the world a better place and to do good things as best we can while helping people with whatever gifts we were given. Instilling those values in your own nuclear family and helping them realize how lucky and blessed we all are is important for me. The same goes for realizing nothing is given to you; you get your butt in gear and earn it.

When I work with successful people who aren't boastful but instead, are reserved givers who are modest about their achievements and their actions, I am instantly inspired to help them plan for their ideal retirement. If a relationship between us is struck in our initial meeting, The Fresh Approach, we can then move forward, and they become my clients.

The Fiduciary Standard

When I can tell a relationship will work out with potential clients who agree to let me prepare a financial retirement plan for them, an explanation of the fiduciary standard is in order.

More and more people have learned the definition in recent years because of mounting criticism charging the broker-dealer community with putting clients into investments that are not suitable for them. The SEC approved a "Regulation Best Interest" package in June 2019. This reform required broker-dealers to disclose conflicts of interest, though it still falls short of the fiduciary standard.[2] The fiduciary standard binds me, legally and ethically, to put your best interests before mine.

I have no selling agreement I must meet for a parent company nor any sales manager pushing me to sell certain investments.

Clients must know, too, that I am compensated, so I earn a percentage of the assets under management rather than earn commissions based on sales. My fee covers research, analysis, due diligence, trading, outside audits, and anything else necessary for Murray Financial Group to adequately assess, execute, and manage investments.

Realize, too, that advisors should be aligned with reputable financial custodians. They should not be transferring your funds into their personal or corporate bank accounts, nor should they be asking you to write checks directly to the advisor for any investments they make. We use TD Ameritrade, Pershing, and AssetMark Trust as our custodians. The presence of a third-party custodian for your investments provides

---

[2] Bob Pisani. CNBC. June 6, 2019. "A breakdown of whether investors are safer after the SEC passes financial protection rule." https://www.cnbc.com/2019/06/06/a-breakdown-of-whether-investors-are-safer-after-the-sec-passes-financial-protection-rule.html

an extra, essential level of accountability to ensure your money is where it's supposed to be.

Chapter Two

Great Expectations

T hink for a moment about a television commercial depicting retirement. Does golf come to mind? Maybe a shot of a couple smiling triumphantly after one of them knocked in a putt?

For some, sharpening the golf game sounds captivating in their golden years. Many retirees do just that, improving their handicaps while maintaining or developing a network of friends.

Consider this quip, though, about the game so many believe will occupy them virtually every day in retirement:

"Golf is played by twenty million mature American men whose wives think they are out having fun." The quote is attributed to the late Jim Bishop, a syndicated columnist and author of biographical accounts and Christian-themed books.

Chances are good that, at some point, men inform their wives that golf—an endeavor subject to frequent futility—is barely tolerable some days. Perhaps women who play golf inform their husbands of that very epiphany.

Many a client has told me of their intentions to play. They do so shortly after retiring but often find that golf can be unforgiving. Find a swing that blasts the ball long and straight off the tee and, bam, you feel like you could chip better with a rake than a wedge.

One client, Larry, absolutely loved golf. He told me so repeatedly, long before he retired. Throughout his work career, Larry's opportunities to play were sporadic. Commitments at work or with family kept Larry from booking regular tee times. But he always wondered what it would be like to have that flexibility with an open schedule.

"Man, you know, Chris, I can't wait to retire. I'm going to play golf every day if I can," Larry told me during the second phase of our planning process, "Great Expectations." As retirement commenced, Larry got in eighteen holes quite often. Occasionally he'd squeeze in another nine if a playing partner was receptive.

Larry's devotion to golf, however, did not last. The novelty wore off. Larry grew tired of being at the course. He didn't quit playing golf, though he desperately needed something else to provide him some fulfillment: A challenge.

Larry's daughter and son-in-law happened to own a bus company.

"Why don't you drive a school bus for me?" the son-in-law asked.

Larry didn't think long and hard about the offer. Why not? The hours weren't bad. He was an early-riser, so getting kids off to school fit his schedule. Same for carting them home in the late afternoon. Summers provided downtime with school out. Besides, the nature of the business allowed him to help his daughter's family.

Not long after he started, Larry discovered the job to be one of the best moves he could make. In the back of his mind, he knew he could quit anytime or ask his son-in-law to find a substitute on days he wanted to reconnect with friends at the golf course and fill out a foursome.

That rarely happened, though. The interaction Larry shared with the middle-school kids delighted him and even piqued his curiosity. He lit up anytime he began telling stories about his riders, even when they misbehaved. "I'll just jerk the bus off to the side of the road," he said, "and tell them, 'Hey, settle down, sit in your seat, or I'll yank you right off this bus.'"

Until then, no bus driver ever said that to them. Or, at least, none who had bothered to stop the bus. Now, of course, Larry did not intend to send kids scrambling to the curb dragging their backpacks. But he commanded their attention while trying to keep himself from laughing out loud at times.

Larry didn't have a care in the world. His daughter or son-in-law wouldn't dare fire him, and, if either did, so be it.

It turned out the relationships Larry established with those kids were purposeful. He cared deeply about them, got to know them by name, and learned their backgrounds and interests. As he continued driving kids to and from school, the times he threatened to jerk the bus to the side of the road diminished. Unless he really did want to laugh out loud. By then, the kids laughed along with him.

Anytime someone tells me they want to spend retirement playing golf or goes on and on about a singular endeavor they want to pursue, I think of Larry. Sometimes I bite my tongue.

But just as frequently, I'll pose a somewhat pointed question: "Well, besides that, or, if you get bored by that, is there any type of charitable work or social work you'd like to do?"

If they haven't spoken much about traveling to see family members, I'll ask if that's a possibility in retirement. Or, simply taking vacations to destinations they've always wanted to visit.

Besides, if a client retires in Frederick or the surrounding Mid-Atlantic region, they're not going to play golf here 365 days a year. On average, Frederick receives forty-plus inches of annual rainfall. In addition, freezing temperatures are the norm in December, January, and February. If golf is on the winter agenda, it's going to happen at a heated driving range or somewhere south of here.

I have clients who book such golf trips or are "snowbirds" who winter elsewhere. Others, however, live here year-round. For any and all of them, finding their purpose—much like Larry did driving a school bus—is critical in retirement. Retirement becomes your reward when purpose becomes your passion.

The Balancing Act

The accumulation of wealth only facilitates retirement. You're still alive, thus you still must remain active. If not, days drag on incessantly.

Much like golf may not be the end all-be all, neither is a favorite television program, a series of books written by a favorite author, or a restful spot rocking on the deck or in a recliner. . .even, believe it or not, if that easy chair is located on or near the beach.

An article from caniretireyet.com asserts that a balanced life portfolio must focus on four key principles: health, people, pursuits, and places.[3]

While it is a significant adjustment to follow a budgetary plan designed to preserve wealth, the lifestyle adjustment retirees experience can be equally challenging. Hobbies are essential. Often, clients spend additional time on hobbies they enjoyed for years. But they often acquire new hobbies, too. These can involve new acquaintances who become friends and create an entirely new social network.

Hobbies, in fact, composed the last ninety-four possibilities in an exhaustive list of "120 Big ideas for What to Do in Retirement," an essay written for newretirement.com by Kathleen Coxwell. The list includes potential hobbies alphabetized from A to Z, beginning with activism and ending with Zumba.[4] The article floats intriguing ideas about what to do in retirement and concludes with this inquiry: "Describe your ideal day. Would you want to do this every day? Could you?"[5]

---

[3] Darrow Kirkpatrick. caniretireyet.com. April 1, 2019. "Reasons to Live: Finding Your Purpose after Retirement or Financial Independence." https://www.caniretireyet.com/reasons-to-live-finding-your-purpose-after-retirement-or-financial-independence/

[4] Kathleen Coxwell. newretirement.com. March 28, 2019. "120 Big Ideas for What to Do in Retirement." https://www.newretirement.com/retirement/what-to-do-in-retirement/

[5] Ibid.

Obviously, this is a question to begin analyzing prior to retirement. Which is why, during a second visit with clients, I hope to at least get them thinking about what it is they want to do, and try, in retirement.

Hopefully, their answers are more elaborate than simply playing golf. If, by now, you are still consumed by the prospect of getting in eighteen holes (or more) every day in retirement, realize, too, that many professional golfers are adversely affected by back and joint pain as they age.

I can attest to such ailments. I raced motocross into my early twenties, then straddled my motorcycle again when my sons became interested in racing. One nasty spill in my early forties put me in the hospital with both a fractured and compressed lower lumbar. Put simply, I broke my back.

Intensive rehabilitation contributed to my full recovery, but I don't wish back pain—even the nagging variety—on anyone.

The sooner aspiring retirees begin thinking in real terms about what it is they want to do with the additional time they'll have, the easier it is to budget for those desires. We then must decide if their wishes are affordable within the retirement plans I construct. I attempt to build plans that assure clients their funds will last into their nineties at least.

That inclination to work in a garden center or begin an in-home business is hypothetical until you actually begin working in that capacity. Then you must determine if you like the work.

Sometimes the prospect of supplemental income in retirement just doesn't pan out. Realizing that, I ask clients: "If you don't earn additional income after you leave the full-time workforce, will you be okay in retirement and not outlive your money?"

This, after all, is the question everyone wants resolved when they consult a financial retirement advisor.

Do I have enough money to retire on? Moreover, will I outlive my retirement income?

However, aspiring retirees also need to know it's unrealistic to assume each day is going to be spent doing nothing. Whether it's grandkids to visit, trips to take, honey-do's to tackle, or, yes, golf to be played, retirement requires income.

A proper plan must be built to allow for expenses, taxes, and inflation while providing income and growth through investments. Following a plan, and the budget established within it, helps prevent a devastating revelation a few years into retirement. Then is not a good time to say, "Wow, I'm putting a big dent into all of my savings, and it's not going to last me even ten more years."

So, then, the exotic vacations you wish to take, the airfare to visit friends or relatives, or the outlay needed to see America in a motor home must be incorporated into the plan as future expenses.

By doing so, anyone closing in on potential retirement should begin thinking harder about just what it is they want to do in retirement. When they evaluate future expenses and notice that money could get really tight as they age, prudent people will re-evaluate, make a few alterations to their aspirations, and let me take a crack at stretching their retirement dollars a bit further.

Age-Defying Statistics

Life expectancy calculations for those living in the United States, compiled from data examined by the Centers for Disease Control and Prevention, do not always paint a rosy outlook. Life expectancy in our country actually began to decline in the late 2010s.

The average age of death for Americans was 78.6, according to a report the CDC released in November 2018. The decline, though not drastic, was believed to be caused to some extent by drug overdoses that typically claim younger citizens and the obesity epidemic that has affected America as well as developed countries in Europe.[6]

These factors are painfully disturbing. Nonetheless, it is important to distinguish that, throughout the twentieth century, longevity for Americans had trended upward.

Medical advancements, coupled with modifications in lifestyle, nutrition, and exercise, contributed to gains in mortality rates. One in forty Americans died annually in 1900 compared to one in 140 in 2013.[7] Socioeconomic factors are often cited, too, in differing rates of mortality among ethnic groups in the U.S. Health factors, some related to genetics, also play a role in when people die.

One interesting remark I once incorporated into the first half of *Your Financial Editor* came from Olivia S. Mitchell, the executive director of the Pension Research Council at the Wharton School of Business.

"Longevity is increasing around the world faster than many of us can fathom," Mitchell said. "In fact, demographers say the baby who will live to be 200 has already been born. This perspective can make insurance and health care providers blanch, as most are not yet thinking about how to manage truly consequential longevity risk."[8]

That prospect certainly creates some intriguing dilemmas associated with preparing for retirement.

As it is, however, we just don't know when our time is up. So, even if you don't plan to be around for your 200th birthday, it is best to prepare conservatively for retirement.

---

[6] Olga Khazan. The Atlantic. Nov. 29, 2018. "Americans Are Dying Even Younger." https://www.theatlantic.com/health/archive/2018/11/us-life-expectancy-keeps-falling/576664/

[7] Penn Wharton. University of Pennsylvania. July 27, 2016. "Mortality In The United States: Past, Present, and Future." https://budgetmodel.wharton.upenn.edu/issues/2016/1/25/mortality-in-the-united-states-past-present-and-future

[8] Wharton University of Pennsylvania. Knowledge@Wharton. July 22, 2019. "Living Longer, Saving Less: What it Will Mean for Retirement." https://knowledge.wharton.upenn.edu/article/preparing-for-retirement/

****

The conversation about death is unpleasant. Some of my clients never planned to assess mortality factors or speak frankly about death to anyone. When their time comes, it comes. Others believed they can accurately estimate their arrival time at the Pearly Gates.

One client seemed so certain I almost wondered if he already called the mortuary to book the funeral and the newspaper to reserve space for his obituary. For the sake of full disclosure, we had been friends for years, and we kidded each other all the time.

When the life-and-death conversation arose, he didn't hesitate. "I'm done in ten years," he stated.

He wanted to sound convincing because he truly wanted me to build a retirement plan that would allow him to exhaust his funds in ten years.

"So you're going to spend all your money in that time?" I asked. "You might still be here, man."

"No, I'm not going to be around after ten years," he responded.

"There's nothing really wrong with you," I said. "That's pretty short-sighted, brother."

Eventually, I talked him off the ledge he was sure would crumble in a decade. I did so by emphasizing family obligations and hardships he could create if he blew approximately $200,000 annually in order to become penniless at the end of his self-imposed deadline (no pun intended) but then lived longer than he expected.

Obviously, people look at the future, and their time in it, differently. Yet, I always attempt to persuade them to extend their plans into their nineties because age-defying scientific breakthroughs happen all the time.

The marvels of modern medicine continue to astound us. Pills help treat conditions that affect our vital organs. Advanced therapy and rehabilitation help us recover fully from surgeries. We can replace knees or hips and sometimes exercise more vigorously than we did prior to such procedures.

Occasionally I glance at studies regarding mortality rates and consider the circumstances that affect the various findings. Mostly, however, I go by what I've learned in my own advisory practice. Although exceptions do exist, my clients are living longer, on average, while maintaining active lifestyles for longer periods.

The retirement plans I construct are built for life—the remainder of your life, in fact, as you move into and engage in retirement.

Sadly, some clients passed too soon. But in my experience, most who did enjoyed fruitful retirements that sometimes lasted twenty, thirty, and in some cases, even forty years. Why, some folks spent more time retired than they did working. And I'm not just referencing those fortunate enough to retire young.

Think about your own family. The chances are good that a grandparent, parent, aunt, uncle, or cousin lived long, maybe into their hundreds.

Hopefully they prospered, which is what we attempt to allow for you in plans designed to make your retirement funds last a lifetime.

Chapter Three
Critical Investigation

The sun sparkled on a clear day the morning of September 11, 2001. I took off work that Tuesday. We sat on our back patio enjoying a bit of tranquil relaxation. I remember Carole being pregnant with our daughter, Morgan. Our two boys, Devin and Garrett, bounced around with greater exuberance than usual since we had planned everything around a trip to the Baltimore zoo.

I remember virtually every moment of that day. I seldom go anywhere, anytime, without some remembrance of the date, which brought the worst terrorist attack on United States soil.

To this day, the license plate on my vehicle reads, "SEPT 11."

Preparing for a family outing that morning caused a bit of a household news blackout for us. Usually I keep tabs on the markets and other business developments, both for my own understanding and the hourly business updates I provide on the radio. But our visit to the zoo took precedence that day, so I wasn't doing my typical radio segments.

Then, the phone rang. My office assistant called to ask if I had tuned into the horrific devastation.

"Have you seen it?" she asked.

"Seen what? I'm sitting out back," I responded.

"Go turn the TV on," she said.

I did so and saw one of the towers at the World Trade Center on fire. Thoroughly shaken, I peeked out of our den, informed Carole I wanted to watch a couple of things on TV, and cautioned her that some things might be happening that didn't look good. At that point I didn't want to alarm our whole family by going into great detail.

About that time, fighter jets from Andrews Air Force Base soared overhead, and it seemed our house sat beneath the middle of their flight pattern from Washington D.C. to Camp David. Not long after that, television cameras captured the sequence of another plane striking the second tower. I watched and felt shocked, horrified, and angered.

Reality set in. You sensed something dreadfully wrong unfolding as part of an attack on the United States. Anyone who watched remembers where they were and what they were doing.

As I sat on the edge of the sofa, I looked over my right shoulder and saw our oldest son, Devin, just standing there behind me. Looking at his expression, I could tell he sensed my concerns and my agitation just from watching me react. He was only four, but he was obviously affected by what transpired.

I gave Devin a hug and turned off the TV. We all went back outside and let the emotions kind of sweep us into idle thought and reflection. We canceled the trip to the zoo and eventually walked over to my brother's house, swam in the pool that day, and just chilled out.

Yet, my mind raced. As a financial planner, I naturally worried about the economic ramifications of the attacks. As a patriot, I became more concerned about the nature of the terrorist plot and those responsible. As an American, I mourned those in the towers and prayed for the safety of the first responders who bravely charged into those buildings. I knew everyone feared for their own safety and mortality.

After Carole and I tucked our boys into bed that night, I wrote a letter I sent by FedEx to all our clients at Murray Financial Group. I did so out of concern for everyone who entrusted us with their hard-earned money. I did so recognizing clients feared the panic that might spread and impact the markets. I wanted them to realize we would work to get through any financial crisis together through careful evaluations and solid planning.

I also worried about their safety and the safety of all Americans. I wrote in my letter that I did not believe the markets would open until the following week. That proved correct, though the Dow Jones Industrial Average suffered a 7.1 percent drop, with a record decline of 684 points, after the markets reopened. By the end of that week, the DJIA had fallen by 14.3 percent. The 1,369.7-point drop represented the largest one-week decline in history up to that point, prompting stocks to lose $1.4 trillion in valuation.

Despite that economic impact, a level of triumph arose from renewed trading. Looking back, the moment is among the many that proved America would defy the terrorists.

Remember when President George W. Bush appeared at Yankee Stadium to throw out the first pitch at Game 3 of the World Series, just six weeks after the attacks?

Bush rejected a suggestion raised because of security concerns in the Bronx. Rather than appear at a game in Arizona, where the Yankees opened the Series against the Diamondbacks, our Commander in Chief insisted he be in New York.[9] His appearance near Ground Zero proved comforting, and the perfect strike the president lobbed across home plate lifted all our spirits as the New York crowd roared its approval.

With flights on the East Coast grounded after the 9/11 attacks, business for the trains bustled. I always prefer going into New York by train, catching the Acela Express that Amtrak runs from BWI International into Penn Station.

---

[9] Timothy McGuirk. 9/11 Memorial & Museum. Oct. 30, 2018. "Remembering President George W. Bush's 2001 World Series Pitch."
https://www.911memorial.org/connect/blog/remembering-president-george-w-bushs-2001-world-series-pitch

MURRAY FINANCIAL GROUP, INC.
Registered Investment Advisors

220 North Market Street
Third Floor
Frederick, Maryland 21701
301.682.9876 / 888.682.9876
301.682.9878 Fax
Email: murray.advice@erols.com
Website: murrayfinancialgroup.com

Christopher A. Murray, CFS, President

Advisory Board*
David O. Godwin, Jr., Esquire
Montedonico, Hamilton & Altman, P.C. - Frederick, MD
Douglas Boyle, CPA, Managing Partner
Boyle & Biggs - Frederick, MD
Thomas Atkins, Regional Consultant
AssetMark Investment Services - Washington, D.C.

September 11, 2001

Dear

    I ask that you join me for a moment to reflect on how valuable and cherished life is. The financial information I am about to review is overshadowed by the loss of human life, severe and minor injuries as well as the physiological impact that the terrible events in New York City, Washington D.C and Pennsylvania have had.

    However, you have entrusted your wealth to me and you need to know that from the beginning of the terrorist attacks I have been closely monitoring and trying to gauge the potential effects on your investment portfolio. I would like to share some historical information that may prove relevant in the coming days, weeks and months. In December of 1990 by many accounts the economy was in a recession, corporate earnings were weak and a war with Iraq seemed imminent. Sound familiar? We may not be in a "technical recession", but to many it feels like one, we have been swamped with corporate earning warnings and reports this year and someone is going to pay dearly for the acts of war that were committed.

    My point is that although the S&P 500 was down in 1990, after the issues were realized and resolved, the S&P 500 was up 30.1% in 1991. In the end, the long-term outlook overcame the short-term pessimism and after a disappointing 1990 stocks rebounded. If there is a short-term market reaction to these tragic events, a rebound should follow once investors are able to recover from the shock and sort out the impact on economic fundamentals.

    Also, you are probably wondering when the U.S. markets will re-open. The only thing I can share with you is that I travel to the financial district of New York City on a quarterly basis and I have a hard time envisioning how they could re-open that area by the end of the week due to the emergency workers doing their job as well as the huge amounts of debris in a condensed area. Nevertheless, the markets do need to get back to business as soon as possible and if they do open on Thursday or Friday it would be a showing of America's resolve.

    I want to assure you that I will continue to monitor this situation and will provide additional information, as it becomes available. As always, if you would like to discuss any questions or concerns you may have, please feel free to call my office.

Sincerely,
Murray Financial Group, Inc.

Christopher A. Murray
President

CAM/jmh

INVESTMENT MANAGEMENT, ESTATE & FINANCIAL PLANNING
*Advisory Board members are not employees of or directly affiliated with MFG. Advisory Board does not have access to or provide advice on individual accounts.

The passenger business on the train became so busy, however, that I needed to book a flight for meetings I had in New York. I missed my first flight because of the time needed to wade through long security lines. The delay enabled me to observe a moving moment.

As our plane flew into LaGuardia, the cabin grew silent. The pilot then addressed everyone. "Ladies and gentlemen," he said, "this is my first flight into New York since the 9/11 terrorist attacks." He didn't conceal his emotions. How could he?

I didn't ask him, but he could have been flying another plane that September day. A friend could have been flying one of the hijacked airliners. The pilot then pointed out where the Twin Towers once stood as we all noticed the smoldering ashes at Ground Zero. I couldn't help but detect the solemn silence within the cabin as the plane landed.

My business in New York took me to Standard & Poor's to meet with Dr. David M. Blitzer, the chairman of the S&P Dow Jones Indices. I also had a meeting with the quantitative research team at Goldman Sachs.

You couldn't help but notice the heightened security. Army Reserve guardsmen with military rifles manned the hallways. I showed my identification seemingly every six feet . . . and I happen to be a pasty white guy with blonde hair.

Not once, however, did I consider the ID checkpoints a hassle. Instead, I maintained a great degree of respect for those guardsmen and thought, as I still do, about the many first responders who sprinted into the towers to save lives.

With immense respect, and sadness, I still think about 9/11 a great deal and the immediate response. I also remember how Americans came together in various ways, perhaps to give blood, offer prayers, attend church, or fly the Stars and Stripes. I often wish it did not take such a tragedy to unite Americans or compel them to turn to God only in a time of anguish and despair.

Fine-tuning Risk Tolerance

The 9/11 terrorist attacks and their aftermath are historical markers I will never forget and something that endears me to the first responders and military personnel who risk their lives for all of us, and for their love of country, each and every day.

From a financial standpoint, I mention 9/11 as a moment when all of us felt vulnerable. And yes, 9/11 had an adverse impact on the economy at a time when America also faced the dot.com crash after an extended period of growth stemming from the proliferation of internet companies and the investments they spawned.

This ties to the Critical Investigation phase of The Financial Protector™ process because risk is a potentially devastating problem we evaluate at this stage of retirement and the wealth planning we conduct for clients.

As we age, we want to fine tune our risk tolerance. Those funds you worked so diligently to save over the years should never be squandered. Yet, this is particularly true when nearing retirement because you do not have enough time in your work career to recover if you lose a sizeable chunk of your savings.

Unfortunately, people often do not realize just how much they are exposing themselves to risk. We joke among ourselves sometimes about an amount of money we may have stumbled upon and someone says, "Go put it all on red." As it turns out, many portfolios I examine for risk almost seem as if someone is willing to walk up to the roulette wheel and jeopardize an account with one fateful spin.

Pleasant runs in the stock market make us feel even more bullet-proof. Going back to the dot.com bubble burst in the early 2000s, the market valuations of those technology companies became outrageously inflated. Add dot.com to the company name, it seemed, and voila, the stock price soared.

Investors, including those without much rational experience, noticed. I tell clients, some folks actually quit their jobs and sat at their kitchen tables all day, trading in their pajamas and flip flops while smoking imported cigars.

I suppose that's an exaggeration. Then again, maybe not. Sometimes I wish I could stage a photo, or even a video, that symbolizes a dangerously casual approach toward investing. Perhaps it would be enough to alert investors to exercise caution when financial times seem outrageously superior.

I learned a lot from that particular market fallout and from the Great Recession of 2008. Economists often mention variances in indicators associated with different market corrections, but the impact is rarely different in terms of the financial effects felt by individual investors.

In the case of the dot.com bubble burst around 2001, Alan Greenspan, who was then the chair of the Federal Reserve, commented on differences he noticed in that particular economy. Technologies had been instituted that would, he said, enhance productivity, and investments in such technology would benefit companies. Greenspan indicated that economic period was different.

Same thing with mortgage-backed securities and the fallout in 2008. People thought the market would remain strong because house prices would never go down. Again, that proved incorrect.

My point is everyone should exercise caution anytime presumed experts say the economy "is different this time" because of certain factors. Those words never seem too accurate, and market downturns happen despite perceived differences experts cite.

Respecting the hazards of risk through proper diversification is essential. When diversification of assets is structured properly, clients enjoy a peace of mind that not only comforts them in times of trouble but also in good times—when wise investors are aware that market corrections can arise and quickly short-circuit steady gains.

Realize market corrections, especially when viewed as historic cycles, are not only normal, but also necessary. Such corrections allow our economic system to recalibrate. We then get up off the ground, dust ourselves off, and begin riding the next wave.

During our Critical Investigation, clients are shown different analyses of the risk components in their investments to determine strategies that best align with their goals, both as investors and retirees. We use multiple software tools for portfolio design, which trace characteristics inherent to their risk exposure.

If a scenario can unfold that makes it possible for investments to experience wild fluctuations based on market conditions, they often find the potential losses both startling and disconcerting.

Some rules of thumb gained widespread acceptance among financial planners, though I mostly steer clear of such theories. For example, one generalization takes a person's age and subtracts it from a hundred, leaving a difference that represents the percentage of equities an investor should have in his or her portfolio.

I prefer to start with a simple amount, say $100,000, and ask clients if they are more comfortable risking 2 percent of that figure or would they be amenable to losing between $15,000 and $30,000. Guess what? Most investors prefer smaller percentages to avoid a catastrophic fallout.

We want clients to comprehend what their risk exposure truly means to them and their livelihood and remove any unrealistic expectations or scenarios dispensed by a co-worker, brother-in-law, or neighbor willing to spout opinions.

Frankly, I stay away from generalizations. When preparing a retirement plan, calculations for income and expenses are based on projections of variables (such as inflation and taxes) and depend on assets available. I attempt to build plans that last clients into their nineties. Percentages applied to equity allocations are going to be different based on individual circumstances.

I print risk analysis reports, discuss them with clients and even hand them red pens to make observations about risk variables. I tell them we want to assess their risk tolerance as best as possible, but we can obviously make adjustments, especially after they see potential losses based on market projections.

Man Vs. Machine

While attending our son Devin's commencement exercise upon his graduation from James Madison University, the different types of degrees offered in the mathematics department amazed me.

I could count the number of quantitative math graduates on just two hands as they received their diplomas. Some of these bright minds would probably move on to represent the future of investing. These are mathematicians so skilled at math and coding that they can help produce the algorithms that make artificial intelligence (AI) a cutting edge force capable of continuing to revolutionize investment processes.

In particular, firms that manage hedge funds and private equities rely greatly on AI and the people who can build algorithms capable of processing information at breakneck speed.

Algorithms developed for computer programs used by financial firms can react to trading opportunities faster than the brainwaves possessed by even the smartest investors.

Some estimate that AI contributes to more than half of all S&P 500 trading. But things can go wrong. Faulty computer algorithms may have accelerated a 2018 selloff that contributed to an 800-point decline in the Dow Jones Industrial Average that took only ten minutes.[10]

Advancements have brought us to the point where robo-advisors are available to help with your investment needs. It's conceivable that you might not pay a robo-advisor as much as, say, Chris Murray, for financial services.

---

[10] BBC. Feb. 6, 2018. "Did robot algorithms trigger market plunge?" https://www.bbc.com/news/business-42959755

With that tradeoff, however, comes some inherent issues. For starters, what kind of conversation can you have with a robo-advisor to state your investment goals, determine your risk tolerance, or voice any particular concerns that might factor into ascertaining your sufficient retirement income?

Often, clients I meet with don't know all these answers with absolute certainty. They like to bounce investment ideas off me, or simply listen to ideas I have as a long-time professional in the financial services industry. It's why we're called advisors.

Some kind of questionnaire typically enables a robo-advisor to understand some of your preferences as an investor. Still, that questionnaire likely will not dig deep into variables that are unique to you, a living, functioning human being. Money management often demands someone's ability to speak to you about your specific goals and issues and provide alerts when confronted with market shifts.

For some, trading through the use of a robo-advisor is ideal. For others, especially those who want some context about market reactions and what it means to them, their trust in a human advisor is important. I might even say invaluable when the client doesn't want to be bothered with details about investments but relies on a financial professional to make sound recommendations.

Remember the Hard Times

Most of our investors had money in the market in 2007 to 2009 during the period of the Great Recession. A national survey Bankrate conducted in 2019 revealed 48 percent of respondents noticed no improvement in their financial situation since the beginning of the

Great Recession. Of those polled, 23 percent said their financial situation worsened, despite a decade of recovery.[11]

I cannot say I heard this level of negativity from clients about the fallout they faced from the Great Recession. The dire numbers from the Bankrate survey, however, indicate the level of despair a market collapse can create for Americans aiming too high for market growth without adequate protection.

I want investors to remember how they felt in 2008 and 2009. How did the downturn affect you? Were you scared? Did it negatively impact your health? Did you make poor decisions? Did it create anxiety from worrying about the losses you saw on paper?

I tell them to also remember the dot.com bubble, the crisis stemming from the 9/11 terrorist attacks, and the downturn caused by the coronavirus outbreak of 2020. All were events that buckled everyone's knees. I certainly don't relish those memories, but I respect the lessons learned and suggest that clients think about those moments when assessing their risk profiles.

Many, of course, assume they are not subjected to much risk based on assurances from a proprietary advisor who represents a big-box firm. Now, some of these financial professionals are good people. I previously worked for New York Life Securities and Principal Financial and met many top-rate advisors. They are, however, paid to peddle their own company's products.

A chief financial officer from a car dealership scheduled a visit once with Murray Financial Group and wanted me to review his retirement assets. Between what he did for a living, his guarded nature, and the assurances he received from his brokerage, the accountant thought his investments matched his risk tolerance.

"I'm conservative," he said. "I'm a conservative guy."

---

[11] Sarah Foster. Bankrate. June 13, 2019. "Survey: Nearly 1 in 4 American adults are worse off now than before the Great Recession."
https://www.bankrate.com/personal-finance/smart-money/great-recession-survey-june-2019/

Nothing wrong with that, I thought. He proceeded to inform me he didn't really need the money he invested because of additional funds he would use in retirement, along with his Social Security benefit. Nonetheless, he did not want to take undesirable risks with his investments in case something forced him to use those funds down the line.

Convinced that his portfolio was conservative in nature, he nearly leaped from his seat after I reviewed his statements and characterized his investments as 90 percent equity. A few bonds did little to offset the aggressive tendencies. The portfolio included no corporate CDs nor a fixed rate annuity. With the bulk of his money exposed to equities, the gas pedal was pressed close to the floorboard.

"To me it sounds like it's exactly the opposite of what you want," I said. "Do you think the fella you were seeing didn't really understand what you were saying?"

Suddenly the CFO, an accountant by trade, grew agitated. He realized the big-box firm attempted to recklessly multiply beans he had been content counting. The firm disregarded his instructions to keep things conservative.

"I told him exactly what I wanted," he fumed. "I didn't want to have anything risky. I didn't need to take any chances on growing that money. I just wanted to preserve it and get a bit of return if I could."

Timing worked in the accountant's favor. The unexpected shock I gave him came after the Great Recession, during a period that became the longest bull run in the history of the stock market. The flourish began on March 9, 2009, and the longest run became official on August 22, 2018, with a 3,453rd day of uninterrupted gains.[12]

---

[12] Matt Egan. CNN Business. August 22, 2018. "Market milestone: This is the longest bull run in history." https://money.cnn.com/2018/08/22/investing/bull-market-longest-stocks/index.html

Quickly, he agreed to let me handle his accounts and become my client. I restructured his portfolio to align with his conservative wishes. His anger, as far as any of our visits, remains an isolated instance caused by the portfolio shock that stunned him at our first appointment. I've encountered other instances when clients left big-box firms after confronting unexpected surprises, but the reaction of the otherwise unflappable CFO from the auto dealership is among the most memorable for me.

If clients still want to be aggressive, I will help them do what they want because that is the role clients charge me with. Nonetheless, I suggest building a reserve fund of cash they can access as a backup. When taking on additional risk in a portfolio, it is wise not to make withdrawals from that portfolio and begin selling in a down market. That's when paper losses become real losses. It's best to use liquid assets from a money market fund or certificate of deposit for income when the need to tap another source arises.

Verifying all assets is important at this stage of the planning process.

Sometimes people list only their 401(k) allocation, for example, when they might also be saving money through another mechanism, even if it is to grow their emergency fund. These details are important.

Another couple I worked with initially forgot to mention that they owned a city lot. That lot, nonetheless, was an asset and needed to be listed as such, along with a conservative estimate of its value. When assessing finances, we must gain a total grasp of everything involved before finalizing a plan.

When assessing future expenses, however, I always encourage clients to err on the side of caution and estimate high.

For example, if the estimated cost for veterinary care is listed, it's good to remember that reductions in such expenses are rare. As pets age, they require additional services. Costs imposed by vets typically increase, too, much like anything else.

This potential expense gets me thinking of Diesel, our beloved Labrador at home. We certainly love our pets and know clients do too, while realizing, in retirement, we have time to spoil them even more. We definitely want them to receive the best care possible.

Usually I remind clients at this stage about their wishes to see the world, the country, or the grandkids in retirement. Envision the costs for travel, hotels, food, amusement, and gifts (either for yourselves or others). Have you properly detailed all potential expenses? Think of everything? It's smart to take another look-see at the potential costs of booking planes, trains, and automobiles. Oh, and recreational vehicles, cruise ships, and helicopter tours.

I'm not arguing against any exotic ventures. They're a blast. But expenses should not exceed estimates. Look at this way: If any windfall remains, a quick getaway can become an unexpected delight. Unless you wanted to apply those funds to next year's grand excursion.

Couples Unite

The prospect of a second vacation brings me to a final observation about the Critical Investigation meeting.

When I am advising couples, I become pretty insistent that each spouse attend this meeting.

I know all about one partner handling most financial decisions. What if you're that partner, though, and you pass away first? Do you really want your grieving spouse confused by various financial considerations? Or what if your spouse takes on care-giving responsibilities after you can no longer perform activities of daily living such as bathing, continence, dressing, feeding, toileting, and transferring? Do you really want your spouse to care for you and also fret about paying bills and withdrawing funds from the correct accounts?

Believe me, it is best that the couple, not just one person, gains an understanding of the retirement plan I construct—if for no other reason than we all get to know each other. Even if the person who doesn't handle the finances cares little about the conversation, there can always be something that strikes his or her interests.

I feel I can provide a calming influence for widows, in particular, during the difficult period that follows a spouse's death. That level of comfort and trust is expedited if she already knows me to some extent.

In addition, it just makes sense for the couple to feel "whole" about their financial arrangements. When another party (in this case, me) becomes involved, everyone needs to hear each other out and comprehend final considerations leading into the formation of a retirement plan.

I attempt to build retirement plans to last a lifetime, which means the person most impacted is the spouse who lives the longest.

Chapter Four

A Panoramic Picture

Relationships I have developed with clients who arrange time to consult with me often develop organically.

I feel as if I scrammed from the "wholesale" side of financial planning when I opened Murray Financial Group and became an independent fiduciary no longer tied to proprietary products. So, I guess I tend to cite the "organic" beginnings to many relationships I enjoy with clients. I will say, though, that many of those meetings—and the friendships they create—are quite dear to me.

One couple we worked with to customize a retirement plan illustrates the "panoramic picture" our firm provides, based on the assets within their portfolio, the clients' risk profile, and the vision they articulated to us regarding their specific retirement desires.

After Carole gave birth to our first child, Devin, he began having some problems eating. Shannon, our maternity nurse at the hospital, learned where we lived and volunteered to swing by if Devin experienced difficulties eating after we took him home. Sure enough, Devin struggled to eat, so I called Shannon and she gladly came over to our house and helped out.

Carole delivered all our children at the same hospital, and after Shannon learned I worked as a financial advisor, she informed other nurses. I helped several of them, primarily with rolling over their 403(b) plans, which are retirement accounts for employees of public schools and tax-exempt organizations.

The financial situation Shannon and her husband Ray presented is especially memorable for me.

Ray was a Vietnam veteran who lost a limb in the war. After returning home, Ray found work with a defense contractor. Shannon related some of her concerns about retirement planning to me one day. I told her to swing by the office with Ray, and I would look at their finances.

It proved to be a scattershot of various documents and paperwork, with numbers they didn't fully grasp. Shannon told me they needed some assistance organizing and understanding different accounts. Truer words could not have been spoken, though I managed to give them an overview of everything and eventually tied it all together into a retirement plan.

The strategies included Shannon's 403 (b) plan and its rollover when she retired from the hospital. At about that same time, Ray retired, partly because his back increasingly stiffened from his work commute and the effects caused by his artificial limb.

Sadly, Shannon passed away. Before her funeral, Ray popped into the office. I think he wanted to get out and have a little time on his own yet still wanted some company. I tried to comfort him and reassured him to remain diligent in following the plan I prepared, which included survivor contingencies. He told me of plans for Shannon to be laid to rest in Arlington National Cemetery and that he would join her there eventually.

His comments that day really touched me, especially after he could see that things would work out financially. He could see how the plan they followed would even enable him to leave money to their kids and grandkids when he passed.

They were just the perfect clients you would like to stick on a copy machine and reproduce a thousand times. Great people, Shannon and

Ray, willing to lend a hand anytime, beginning with the nursing skills and instincts Shannon possessed. She helped ease the tension and uncertainty we faced as first-time parents.

The Panoramic Picture meeting is designed to introduce financial instruments and benefits used in retirement. During this segment of our process, circumstances identified in the Critical Investigation are tied together into a collective piece that provides a structured approach to life in retirement.

Social Security

Clients regularly ask questions about the viability of Social Security. After all, life expectancy in the United States has experienced steady increases since the system was enacted in 1935.

The Social Security Administration concedes "increases in life expectancy are a factor in the long-range financing of Social Security; but other factors, such as the sheer size of the 'baby boom' generation, and the relative proportion of workers to beneficiaries, are larger determinants of Social Security's future financial condition."[13]

Everyone recognizes acute problems. Gloomy issues are stated in black and white each year when the trustees of the Social Security and Medicare trust funds release reports detailing the current and projected status of the two federal programs and the pending insolvency of each.

Realizing the gridlock that often grips Washington, politicians will wait until roughly the two-minute warning before attempting a concerted effort aimed at fixing the problems.

I tell baby boomers who express concerns about Social Security that benefits they begin collecting will probably be there in retirement. If a baby boomer mentions some click-bait out there that scares them about Social Security, I tell them I don't think it's going to happen.

---

[13] SSA.gov. "Social Security History." https://www.ssa.gov/history/lifeexpect.html

If politicians took away all senior citizen programs or Social Security, or even enacted a major reduction, everyone would revolt and go after them with pitchforks.

Younger citizens could be in jeopardy of losing benefits similar to what their parents and grandparents received. Eventually (an undefined expression of time when it comes to politics), some sector of our society—Generation X? Millennials?—should expect some potential cuts to Social Security.

When examining Social Security, the first move is for clients to access the ssa.gov website to learn the current estimates of their benefits. I encourage clients to make an appointment with a representative at the Social Security office, too. While the clerks are not allowed to dispense advice, they can provide direct answers to questions.

We know how projected benefits can fit into future planning for clients. If adequate income exists from other sources, often the wise decision is to delay accepting Social Security benefits until the maximum age of seventy.

Between full retirement age and the age of seventy, benefits increase 8 percent every year someone defers taking them. Eight percent is a good rate of return and something to take advantage of if someone is in a good position to do so.

However, family health history and any chronic health issues clients face also play into the decision of when to claim a Social Security benefit.

Uncertainty creeps in any time someone attempts to project their life span. Still, if enough warning signs exist to suggest someone may not live a long, healthy retirement, it is usually in their best interest to begin collecting Social Security sooner to take advantage of the benefit plan they paid into once the mandatory FICA deduction was imposed on a paycheck they earned.

Considering when to take Social Security requires a structured approach that balances both financial and health factors. The decision is something of a crapshoot since no one can accurately predict their mortality.

Clients who retire early, say around fifty-five, obviously could leave the workforce after making a nice living. With them, we analyze methods to allow them to live off their savings. Then, when they turn sixty-two, they begin collecting Social Security to stabilize the reduction of other assets and to allow them to set aside funds for legacy plans.

The kicker to this is if someone wants to work part-time but collects Social Security before their full retirement age. In such cases, they cannot earn more than $18,240 annually based on the limit imposed in 2020 or their Social Security benefits will be reduced.[14]

Once they reach their full-time retirement age, they can pocket unlimited earnings. Of course, some who enjoy what they do and have no desire to retire can work until they turn seventy and then gain their maximum Social Security benefit. After turning seventy, Social Security benefits no longer escalate, so everyone should plan to turn on the spigot by then.

One important note that I stress to couples about Social Security is the void that will be left after one spouse passes away. The surviving spouse can collect the larger of the two benefits but should still be aware, and prepared, for a reduction in income derived from Social Security.

Medicare

Assumptions are not entirely bad when planning for retirement. For example, everyone has an idea of what an ideal retirement might

---

[14] Dan Caplinger. The Motley Fool. Jan. 24, 2020. "Your 2020 Guide to Working While on Social Security." https://www.fool.com/retirement/2020/01/24/your-2020-guide-to-working-while-on-social-securit.aspx

incorporate, but once you get into that time of life, you may find something in particular takes precedence. That's one reason it is always prudent to review every part of the plan to make sure we account for all variables.

Unfortunately, some assumptions can be dead wrong. One of the worst mistakes made by any retiree is the misconception that the government will take care of all health issues and thinking it's unnecessary to project health care expenses.

Medicare and Medicaid are the two health insurance programs offered through the government. While each can provide great assistance for health care in retirement, they do not usually cover all of your medical costs.

Those who paid into the system for at least ten years are eligible for Medicare enrollment.

I cannot stress enough that you must enroll during the three-month period prior to turning sixty-five. While you have the three months before your sixty-fifth birthday and the three months after, those who fail to comply with this deadline could risk paying increased premiums for the remainder of their lives.

Medicare covers those sixty-five and older and is split into parts. Part A is hospital insurance derived from funds paid through payroll taxes and usually does not require a premium. Part B is medical insurance. Part C is Medicare Advantage, which combines coverage provided through Parts A and B into one private plan and often includes prescription drug coverage. Part D is prescription drug coverage.[15]

Medicare does not cover long-term care generated by dementia or the move into a nursing home based on inability to perform ADLs (activities of daily living)—feeding, dressing, bathing, transferring, toileting, and walking.

---

[15] medicaremadeclear.com. March 31, 2020. "Medicare Basics"
https://www.medicaremadeclear.com/basics

Other options that also impose premiums are available as Medicare Supplemental Insurance. Costs and limitations vary by carrier with these plans, which are again split into different parts—F, G, H, I, J, etc.

Medicaid includes more limitations because its administration by states results in more variance in terms of funding and protocol. Medicaid typically kicks in when someone exhausts most of their income. Those who need nursing home care and possess more assets than the Medicaid limit in their state will have to use their assets first to pay for care.[16]

While I consult with clients about the basics of Medicare and Medicaid, I also instruct them to educate themselves by checking out www.Medicare.gov and www.Medicaid.gov. Each website instructs readers on state and federal rules imposed. Also, I refer clients to other advisors who specialize in offering Medicare supplements that can help cut medical costs and provide financial protection in retirement.

For those who consider retiring before turning sixty-five, remember, Medicare does not kick in until your sixty-fifth birthday in the vast majority of cases. Vanguard, for instance, reports that median costs from marketplace health care coverage average $12,800 per person at age sixty-four compared to $5,200 in annual costs when Medicare becomes available at age sixty-five.[17]

Pensions

To some, pensions may seem as outdated as watching television on a black-and-white set that needs its rabbit ears adjusted just right to generate clear images. For those who don't remember such

---

[16] Ibid.
[17] Vanguard: Living in Retirement. Feb. 20, 2019. "How much does retirement health care cost?" https://investornews.vanguard/how-much-does-retirement-health-care-cost/

technological relics, or, for that matter, an episode of *The Virginian*, it's possible a pension seems just as outdated.

Many corporations eliminated pensions in favor of employees using their own initiative and wherewithal to generate retirement savings through 401(k) options.

Those who do have access to pension plans must make serious observations regarding the overall quality of that pension. An ongoing problem has been the inability of companies and governments to properly fulfill pension obligations with adequate funding.[18]

In addition, the incentivization of lump-sum payouts of pensions is something companies and governments could very well continue as an attempt to reduce payment liabilities. Clients frequently present situations in which they must make decisions regarding lump sum offers.

In the region where we located Murray Financial Group, not far from Washington D.C., government pensions remain an attractive source of retirement income. These pensions, coupled with those still offered in the private sector, are components in many of the retirement plans we construct.

A defined-contribution plan for federal employees, the Thrift Savings Plan (TSP), is built on funds the government employee allocates, along with agency contributions based on eligibility. Those who are covered by the Federal Employment Retirement System (FERS) participate in a three-tier package that includes a FERS basic annuity and Social Security in addition to a TSP.

We consider it wise in most cases for clients to roll out their TSP as a lump sum then invest and protect it properly so they can access the entire amount if necessary. Different circumstances lead to different

---

[18] John Mauldin. *Forbes*. May 20, 2019. "The Coming Pension Problem Is So Big That It's A Problem for Everyone."
https://www.forbes.com/sites/johnmauldin/2019/05/20/the-coming-pension-crisis-is-so-big-that-its-a-problem-for-everyone/#44c47c637fc5

decisions. Some clients choose to annuitize the lump sum, which provides regular income but little control over that big pile of money.

An important aspect about pensions is to understand various options and realize, once a decision is made to begin tapping a pension benefit, it's much like Social Security—there's no turning back.

The financial impact on a surviving spouse is an important consideration. One retiree I advise named Don retired from local government and gladly accepted a lower payment amount from his pension so that if he died before his wife, she would receive 100 percent of his pension.

That, however, is not the desire of every couple. A federal government employee, George, who came to see us before retiring flat out stated he was taking his pension. As a point of clarification, since his wife came in with him, I asked, "Are you going to do the joint survivor's benefit so there's 50 percent or more left for Rachel if you die?" He quickly shook his head and said, "No."

Rachel is roughly ten years younger than George. She worked in the law profession, had previously engaged in a successful law practice, and had no intention of retiring close to when he did. In the case of some couples, an arrangement would have been made to enact the joint survivor's benefit. But George and Rachel previously discussed their situation and mutually agreed to their intentions, even if it meant the husband wanted "to get out every penny I can" from his pension.

We discussed some life insurance possibilities in case something awful happened right away and constructed a plan based on their desires. Although they didn't have any children, I insisted they needed to keep everyone in mind when making that particular pension decision.

Annuities

Discussions centered on annuities involve a broad array of products some clients are skeptical to pursue.

They comment sometimes that they hate annuities. Occasionally they'll tell me they love annuities. Based on either response, I ask, "Well, what kind of annuities?" That question often generates a blank expression.

Annuities seem shrouded in mystery. In a sense, I feel like a television detective when explaining the roles annuities play in retirement plans. Only, in most television mysteries, little time is spent discussing the who-done-it, so the case takes time to unravel, and a solution is revealed at the end of the program.

In my position as a fiduciary, I avoid subterfuge. I do not want annuities to cause confusion. I try to explain the general scope up front. Since annuities are distributed by insurance companies, the instrument can be juxtaposed to life insurance.

People take out life insurance policies to protect finances and beneficiaries upon their death. With annuities, people use the instrument as insurance in case of a long life. Annuities offer financial protection by providing reliable income payments.

An annuitant pays an insurance company an amount in exchange for the company's contractual guarantee it will pay you income for a specified period of time. The annuity contract negotiated with the insurance company determines how long and how much money the company pays.

The point when the income stream is activated is when the contract is annuitized. If the person holding the policy lives longer than the insurance company planned, that company is still obligated to pay out, even if the payments exceed the contract's actual value. Depending on the contract type, however, the insurance company may keep money used to fund the annuity if the holder of the policy dies an untimely death.

Again, this is a simplified definition written to provide a basic concept of annuities, which contain different forms and features. Following are various types of annuities:

Immediate: Money is given to an insurance company in a lump sum up front and payments begin immediately. Once payments begin, the annuitant no longer can access the money in a lump sum and the transaction is irreversible. Upon death, the insurance company retains any remaining contract value.

With other annuity types, contracts are *deferred*, which means a policy is funded as a lump sum over a period of years and is allowed an opportunity to earn interest and grow for years—sometimes even decades. Immediate annuities are considered unfavorable because no opportunity exists to grow the lump sum initially allocated.

Variable: The contract owner can use mutual funds, referred to as sub-accounts, which makes the variable annuity different from other types because it is subject to losses resulting from market declines.

The value of the contract is also subject to fees and limitations of the underlying investment. These can include mortality costs and management fees. Income paid under the contractual terms of the contract is locked in at the value of the contract if annuitized.

Fixed: The contract includes a guaranteed interest rate. Then, when you want to annuitize the contract, the insurance company will make regular income payments at the payout rate the contract guarantees. The payments continue for the rest of your life and, depending on the contract, the remainder of your spouse's life.

The upside potential is minimal, though the guarantees provided make fixed annuities reliable and sound. The value is easy to calculate based on projected lifetime expectancies of the annuitant because it is not subject to market changes.

Fixed index: These contracts have greater growth potential than traditional fixed annuities, but they also have protection from market downturns. Fixed index annuities contain market-linked contracts, allowing growth within a certain range rather than at a set interest rate.

An external market index such as the S&P 500 is used to credit interest gained in the value of the contract. The insurance company credits the contract based on gains in the S&P 500, for instance, though interest is capped.

Some examples: If interest is capped at 5 percent in a year the S&P gains 3 percent, the value of the annuity increases by 3 percent; if the S&P gains 10 percent, the increased value cannot exceed the 5 percent cap. If the market plunges and reflects negative growth, the contract value will not decrease and the annuitant will not lose gains credited in previous years.

The definitions provided are designed to help broaden your knowledge of annuities. Realize I have been a financial income planner for thirty years. Not once have I ever recommended or executed a variable annuity. The fees, expenses, and risks associated with variable annuities are just too high.

I tend to stick to fixed and fixed index annuities because of their predictability and protection from economic downturns.

These are good instruments to use as a kind of bond-replacement type of allocation, and they often provide more upside because of the equity indexes the insurance companies choose for these annuities. They provide diversification within an asset class through an investment that's protected from a devastating market loss. Clients won't lose any of the funds they started with or have earned to that point. Granted, they will not benefit entirely from a big market gain, but they will still receive the growth allowed by the cap or participation rate

Fixed interest and fixed index annuities are fine tools to use when attempting to restructure portfolios to account for lower risk tolerance. Many clients reach the conclusion they prefer a lower risk tolerance once we look at their accounts and often find they need to safeguard more of their assets.

The upside potential can be attractive, too, even if the cap on a fixed index annuity is 5 percent. Money market accounts and certificates of deposit earn far less, or have for years at the point I am authoring this book, so the fixed interest or fixed index annuity is usually much more preferable.

Many clients, once they become more knowledgeable about fixed interest and fixed index annuities, want to understand more about the moving parts.

At the beginning, though, I tell them an annuity is the scientific liquidation—in the form of regular payments over a period of years—of an asset, or principal, that has been created during life. Again, compare that to a life insurance policy that is designed to create principal upon death.

Inflation

Prices are going to go up, right? It's just the nature of life.

When we plan for inflation, I show clients historical data that covers an entire century. Price increases are rather staggering over that time, and even the percentage increases, though often slight, really add up and result in compound inflation. I like to boil that down, though, and examine a ten- or twenty-year average, since that is often more realistic than, say, incorporating the 7.25 percent average inflation rate for the 1970s.[19]

The average annual inflation rate in the United States of 3.22 percent does not sound overly devastating, but understand, at that pace, prices on consumer goods double every twenty years.[20] That certainly isn't a

[19] InflationData.com. "Inflation and CPI Consumer Price Index 1970-1979." https://inflationdata.com/articles/inflation-cpi-consumer-price-index-1970-1979/
[20] Tim McMahon. InflationData.com. April 1, 2014. "Long-Term U.S. Inflation." https://inflationdata.com/Inflation/Inflation_Rate/Long_Term_Inflation.asp

prospect to ignore entering your retirement, especially when average life expectancy has risen appreciably.

I incorporate an inflation rate of 3 to 4 percent into plans constructed to provide room for clients to keep up with expenses and maintain the lifestyles they want to enjoy.

To emphasize the inflationary adjustments, I could cite increases on some type of grocery item, but I've found the best example is the price of a stamp.

Some remember licking stamps to put on an ordinary envelope. It could be, though, that you only recognize self-adhesive stamps, which were introduced in 1974 when the price of postage cost eight cents.

Anyway, postage for mailing an ordinary envelope rose to more than a half-dollar in 2019. Sometimes we didn't notice the increases much when they came in one- or two-cent increments. Nonetheless, the price of a stamp steadily rose. Now, many gladly pay their bills online to save time and money. Those who still use stamps with any regularity know to stock up on the "forever" variety before another hike in postal rates.

Inflation on most goods and services works in much the same fashion and will be something you absolutely must account for in retirement.

Remember, a general rule of thumb in retirement stipulates you count on needing 75 to 85 percent of the income you previously found necessary before retirement.[21] For all of those base expenses, remember inflation can greatly influence the cost of goods and services.

---

[21] Paula Pant. thebalance.com. June 25, 2019. "What Is Your Retirement Number?" https://www.thebalance.com/what-s-your-retirement-number-453995

Chapter Five

The Enforcer

Don't worry. We strive to create retirement plans that are far from unpleasant. The process of reviewing and revising those plans is called The Enforcer only because we're making sure all the planning, all the tools, and all the mechanisms are consistently performing in a precise manner.

The assets we manage are linked to the risk tolerance we deemed appropriate by making proper adjustments. We rebalance and re-evaluate asset classes where portfolios are exposed.

For example, in a period when international funds slump because developed countries overseas are teetering on recession, we examine whether exposure in those funds needs to be trimmed. If so, allocations are dispersed elsewhere.

International market declines, however, are not going to force us to give up on such funds. Races have different outcomes, different winners, and different losers. Economies, markets, technologies, and geopolitical impacts vary at different times around the globe.

The complexities involved with rebalancing should not cause you to lay in bed at night worrying.

That gets me to thinking about all the marketing funneled into providing you proper sleep. Television ads, newspaper inserts, and website popups frequently advertise various mattresses sold by numerous retailers.

The options amuse me to some extent, especially when accompanied by animated sheep. Some folks, perhaps even yourself, go as far as to find your "perfect sleep," then dial a certain number into your programmable bed to go night-night.

The restful sleep of my clients is something I take seriously. When their heads hit the pillow, I do not want them fretting over whether they are being too aggressive with their portfolio . . . or, for that matter, too conservative. We attempt to find a sweet spot for each client and allocate swings accordingly, though The Enforcer process can detect concerns that allow us to adjust.

This is where a number we assign also fits into your sleep pattern. When we evaluate risk, we carefully weigh your responses and then apply your stated tolerance to profiles ranging from one to six.

Low Risk (Profiles 1 & 2)

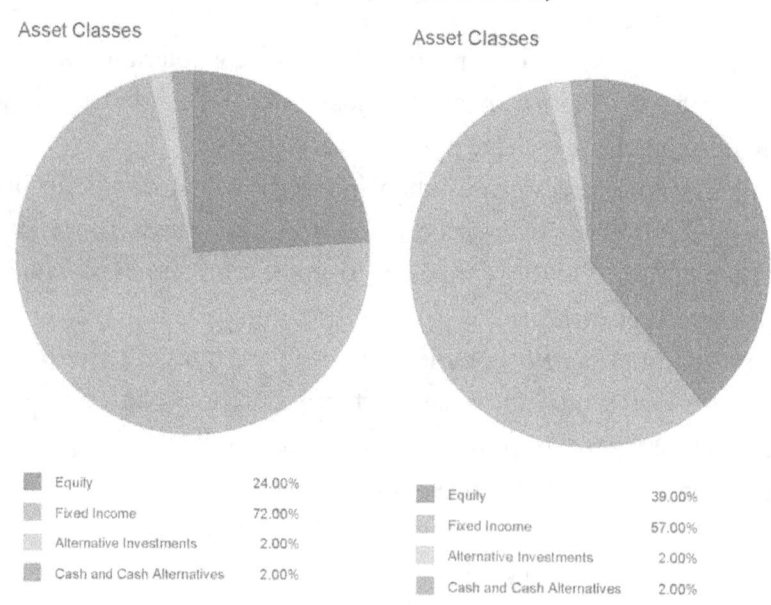

Asset Classes

Equity	24.00%
Fixed Income	72.00%
Alternative Investments	2.00%
Cash and Cash Alternatives	2.00%

Asset Classes

Equity	39.00%
Fixed Income	57.00%
Alternative Investments	2.00%
Cash and Cash Alternatives	2.00%

Medium Risk (Profiles 3 & 4)

Asset Classes

Equity	64.00%
Fixed Income	32.00%
Alternative Investments	2.00%
Cash and Cash Alternatives	2.00%

Asset Classes

Equity	79.00%
Fixed Income	17.00%
Alternative Investments	2.00%
Cash and Cash Alternatives	2.00%

High Risk (Profiles 5 & 6)

Asset Classes

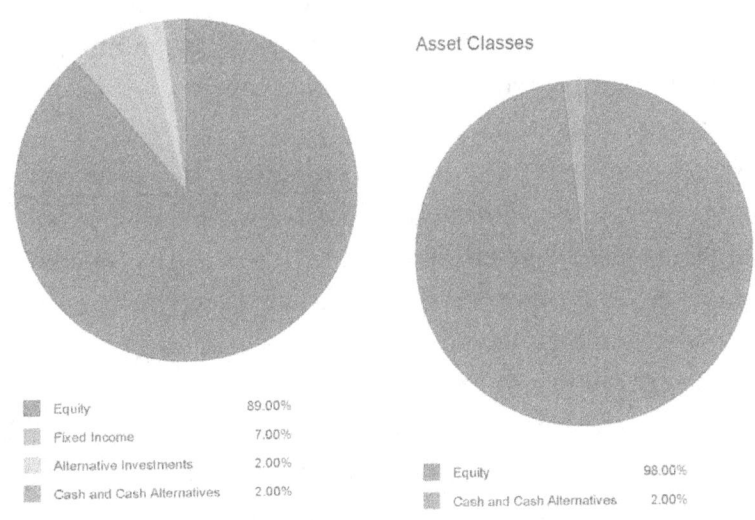

Equity	89.00%
Fixed Income	7.00%
Alternative Investments	2.00%
Cash and Cash Alternatives	2.00%

Asset Classes

Equity	98.00%
Cash and Cash Alternatives	2.00%

Taxing Proposition

Maryland can be an expensive place to live, especially so in Frederick County where my office is located, and also in neighboring counties such as Howard, Montgomery, and Prince George's. These counties are close to the Washington suburbs, and the sprawl continues to attract affluent residents and landowners the county governments attempt to appease with amenities.

For example, in Howard County, we have parks that include ball fields lined with artificial turf, trails to accommodate walkers, joggers, and cyclists, and pavilions that can be used for gatherings and parties.

Often, these amenities do not cater to older citizens. As we age, we aren't as likely to get out as much and use such facilities.

Sometimes efforts are made to accommodate seniors. I heard of one set of commissioners that approved a park heralded as that county's first collection of pickleball courts. By all accounts, pickleball is a growing sport often popular with seniors. Yet, how many actually play pickleball, and become adept at its adaptations of tennis, badminton, and ping pong? Do the participation levels warrant a complex within a park that costs taxpayers millions of dollars?

I look at my mother, who remains active in social circles and continues to drive into Baltimore to work downtown. She would never benefit from a pickleball facility. In effect, she's getting the raw end of the taxpayer deal with services that are supposedly catered to accommodate seniors. Of course, she's also never going to use "turf" ball fields and either practice or play under the lights.

The expenditures, I tell her, are unfair, especially when I recall that, in my youth, fundraising often paid for field improvements. Coaches, parents, and kids joined together to make that happen and felt good about how they helped facilitate projects that bettered their communities. Sometimes the upgrades essentially boiled down to a bunch of us combing the fields to rid the playing surface of stones and pebbles.

Now, it seems, many team fundraising efforts are geared toward facilitating expensive travel squads that can even limit opportunities for some youth.

One more thing about subsidizing elaborate projects with government funds: It's too difficult to pinpoint exactly what it is people want or desire.

For example, a state-of-the-art stadium penalizes kids who have no intentions of setting foot on that field but instead show an incredible gift for art, music, or theater.

Anyway, I'll push aside that soapbox, though it would fit nicely behind a microphone used to address members of a city council or county commission who seem unconcerned by the effects of rising taxes.

What I stress when clients tell me they could relocate in retirement is assessing the tax structure in the community they are considering.

Kick the tires, speak with people, access news accounts, learn what taxes you will have to pay. Municipal taxes, school taxes, and specialty taxes (a burn tax, for example) can add up fast and nibble, if not chomp, away at the fixed income and rigid budget of a retiree.

Look, three circumstances typically influence decisions to move in retirement—weather, family, and the cost of living. Weather, even with its extremes, can be generalized rather easily. Family togetherness can be assessed based on desires and needs. Cost of living is what can vary greatly in communities throughout the country and even in foreign lands.

If such costs factor into your ability to retire comfortably, doing your homework is worthwhile before moving to an area of the country that could be unaffordable.

Uncle Sam's RMD Appetite

One of the bigger issues retirees face is the bite taxes could take out of the savings they think should be ample for retirement. Most of my clients own a 401(k), IRA, or both. Those who are diligent about saving money sock away a portion of their earnings into such accounts, or something equivalent.

These accounts are tax-deferred. Realize, however, that the word "deferred" does not equate to something that is free. Taxation does not work that way. If a transaction entails funds, it almost always includes taxes. Government entities want their slices and often don't mind asking for a big cut with all the toppings.

So how does the government satisfy its appetite? Through the concept of required minimum distributions (RMDs), which can have disastrous consequences if you forget to account for this particular tax assessment on your traditional retirement account.

Beginning at age seventy-two, Americans are required to withdraw a certain minimum amount every year from their 401(k) or IRA. Failure to do so, or if you do so incorrectly, results in a 50 percent tax penalty on any RMD dispersal you should have withdrawn but did not. This penalty is administered on top of income tax.

The administration of RMDs can make a Roth IRA a favorable alternative. Taxes on Roth IRAs are paid on the front end, much like a sales tax is imposed on, say, furniture you purchase.

Early withdrawals on the principal, or on the growth of the Roth IRA after you reach fifty-nine-and-one-half, are not subject to taxes, particularly those enforced by dreaded RMDs. A Roth account must be owned for a minimum of five years before all of its features can be realized.

Contributions to a Roth IRA are bound by a cap, which in 2020 totaled $6,000 for an annual contribution. Those fifty and over are allowed an additional $1,000 in contributions. The amount applies to all traditional and Roth IRA accounts collectively, although it does not limit the amount you can convert from traditional accounts to their Roth counterparts.

Each wealth and retirement plan I construct is different, simply because each client faces different circumstances. In most cases, a blend of pre-tax accounts, such as a 401(k) and traditional IRA, and post-tax accounts (Roth 401(k) and Roth IRA) is beneficial.

No tax on the front end can be beneficial to investors who are also building families and must balance the cost of kiddos with other expenses such as mortgage payments. No tax on the back end is welcome relief to those who are no longer in the workforce and are incapable of building a bigger nest egg.

The Tax Cuts and Jobs Act, commonly called the Trump Tax Plan, lowered tax rates and made conversions from traditional IRAs into Roth IRAs more affordable.

However, political winds can always change abruptly. Ever-increasing federal deficits make it likely that tax rates will rise again. That probability makes it wise to incorporate potential tax hikes into retirement planning, though the severity of any increases is, unfortunately, the great unknown in that equation.

Understanding your tax bracket is vital so you can determine the difference between the next lower and higher tax bracket. Decisions such as Roth IRA rollovers and gifting should be based on this information.

Many are surprised, too, when tax bills come due in retirement and they discover that they look much the same as what they did when they earned a paycheck. Remember, your lifestyle typically does not change that drastically in retirement. Lifestyle expenses for travel and entertainment may decrease later in retirement as you age, but that's when expenses related to health care often strike.

Insurance Alternatives

Insurance needs vary depending on circumstances, resulting in various recommendations I make to clients both while they're working and in retirement. A basic outline of different insurance products is in order to provide a better understanding of different tools that can be incorporated into financial planning.

TEMPORARY INSURANCE

Term Life Insurance: As indicated by the word, "term," this type of insurance protects the insured for a specified period of time, typically ten to thirty years. The coverage amount in a private term life insurance plan is chosen by the individual. This type of policy is commonly offered through employers and typically correlates to a certain amount of wages the insured employee earns.

Premiums for term life insurance policies are calculated based on variables such as age, health factors, coverage limits, and the term of the policy. The likelihood of severe health issues increases by age, which makes term life insurance more difficult to obtain and more expensive as one grows older.

One disadvantage to term life insurance is its temporary nature. The end of the contract term curtails a policy the insured may have paid into for, say, thirty years.

PERMANENT INSURANCE

Whole Life Insurance: Advantages to properly structured permanent life insurance policies include a tax-free death benefit, withdrawals through policy loans not subject to income tax, insurance that remains in force as long as premiums continue to be paid, and cash value accumulation guaranteed by the strength of the insurer.

Whole life policies endow at a certain age, such as ninety or one hundred, meaning the cash value equals the death benefit. By living until the maturity date, the owner of the policy will receive the cash value amount in a lump sum. Unplanned tax consequences may arise from such an occurrence, since the death benefit is not paid out to beneficiaries.

Qualifying for a whole life policy requires the applicant to complete a medical questionnaire and possibly a paramedical exam. Information is then sent to an underwriter who determines a premium rate based on the actuarial categories the applicant is placed into.

The cash value of a whole life policy is credited a certain amount based on the guaranteed rate stipulated in the contract. Dividends are sometimes paid to policyholders at the discretion of the company.

Universal Life Insurance: Actuaries determine set rates to cover the costs associated with whole life insurance policies. With universal life policies, however, the contract holder can decide on a flexible premium, leaving them to decide whether to pay a premium that covers future policy expenses or barely covers your current policy expenses. Realize that the internal cost to an insurance company for maintaining a policy increases over time, which is reflected in term life policies by the escalating cost of coverage.

One potential disadvantage to a universal life insurance policy arises when the policy loses enough value that the policy's expenses are no longer covered by minimum premium payments. In such instances, the policy would lapse. Such details are critical to understand before arranging universal life insurance policies.

Indexed Universal Life Insurance: The ability to withdraw the cash value in a policy without paying income taxes, even on the accumulation, remains in effect with an IUL. The difference is accumulation has the potential to increase more cash value using an index such as the S&P 500 or Dow Jones Industrial Average.

Interest credits with an IUL are based on such indices and are accompanied by a floor and a cap. If the market does well, interest is credited to an IUL up to the policy's cap. If the market does poorly, including negative gains, interest is still credited, though the contract floor is often set at 0 percent.

For example, if the contract value contains a cap of 5 percent, the annual interest credit is limited to that value even if the market returns 20 percent. If the market return is negative 20 percent, the floor of zero percent will not result in a decrease in policy value, though charges and expenses will still be deducted from the policy.

The upside to IUL policies is the prospect of potential growth, protection offered from market losses, and a death benefit for beneficiaries. Adverse effects can result, however, from making withdrawals or executing policy loans from an IUL. Again, it is vital to understand the basics to avoid falling behind on premium payments and risking a lapse in the policy.

The importance of life insurance in financial and retirement planning is vital. Our mortality is something we cannot control. An unexpected or premature death can sink a plan, so protection through life insurance is critical.

Variable Life Insurance: Similar to annuities, permanent life insurance has a version where the life insurance policy is directly tied to the performance of the market, meaning the cash value of the policy may increase or decrease in any given year. The insured has the opportunity to use subaccounts (mutual funds) when allocating their cash values. Of course, another benefit includes not having to pay taxes on the increased value, as it is a life insurance policy and therefore the death-benefit is tax-free.

Preparing for the Long Term

As a kid, I had no idea a couple who lived near us would provide a bit of a template for me when I explain the importance of addressing long-term care contingencies into retirement planning.

Mr. and Mrs. Ellis grew some crops and raised sheep on their eighty-acre farm near our home when I was growing up. Mr. Ellis was a veterinarian and Mrs. Ellis a teacher. They took great pride in their work, both professionally and on their land. After Mr. Ellis died, I remember delivering hay and alfalfa to Mrs. Ellis, who continued to raise sheep and take meticulous care of the farm.

This was true even after the Ellis children had moved away. One day when a daughter visited, the girl noticed that Mrs. Ellis had failed to turn off one of the burners on her stove. One slip after another began to happen regularly. The family concluded they could no longer let Mrs. Ellis live on her own.

Sadly, those days had brought the onset of dementia, a devastating affliction that attacks the mind, even though, in the case of Mrs. Ellis, she was still strong as an ox, physically. Her illness, coupled with her strength, proved to be a devastating combination.

The family moved Mrs. Ellis to the Quaker assisted care facility in a neighboring county. At that time, the facility cost $72,000 per year. Although her capacity to recognize relatives faded completely and Mrs. Ellis eventually could not perform any activities of daily living, the vitality left in her body enabled her to live nine years at the home.

Her family retained me to help them devise some level of long-term care protection, but by the time they inquired, it was too late. Nothing could be done to shelter assets, though I recommended a conservative proposal that involved the sale of the treasured farm to help ease the burden of costs related to long-term care.

I tell this story because, if Mrs. Ellis—a smart, strong, resourceful matriarch—could succumb to the ravaging effects of dementia, it can happen to you, me, or anyone.

This is why it is critical to build some piece of coverage into any retirement plan that accounts for long-term care expenses. The annual median cost based on 2019 data for a private, one-bedroom apartment in a Maryland assisted living facility is $51,600. That annual median cost rises to $116,070 for a semi-private room in a nursing home facility.[22]

Life insurance and long-term care insurance analysis is an important phase of our planning process. Using math, science, data, and statistics, we are able to show the potentially devastating impact on your assets and lifestyle resulting from the costs of assisted care.

---

[22] Genworth (conducted by CareScout®). June 2019. "Cost of Care Survey 2019." https://www.genworth.com/aging-and-you/finances/cost-of-care.html

Chapter Six

Relationship Maximizer

Political chatter is common, obviously, in the region where I live. As I wrote this book, the House of Representatives, under control of the Democrats, initiated impeachment proceedings in 2019 against President Donald Trump.

On the radio, both during my hour-long Saturday segment and my morning business updates, I am not bashful about stating my viewpoints, especially regarding the circus that unfolded with those hearings.

So, yes, I understand when clients may be skittish as to how politics influence the markets. Some thought the election of Trump would cause market declines or even a recession. The opposite happened. The markets flourished.

Then, as the impeachment hearings commenced in November 2019, some thought equity benchmarks would plunge. Yet the Dow Jones Industrial Average, the S&P 500 Index, and the NASDAQ Composite Index soared toward, or even exceeded, all-time highs.[23]

---

[23] Mark Decambre. MarketWatch. November 15, 2019. "The stock market heads to record heights even as the Trump impeachment hearings enter a new phase—here's why." https://www.marketwatch.com/story/the-stock-market-heads-to-record-heights-even-as-the-trump-impeachment-hearings-enter-a-new-phase-heres-why-2019-11-13

Even during a time when national politics generated an abundance of showmanship—Democrats spread out ten-wide on the same stage to conduct debates a year out from the November 2020 election, only to have additional hopefuls enter the fray—the political atmosphere did not undermine market growth. Some financial experts labeled the political maneuverings as merely a sideshow.[24]

The Dow eventually tumbled in early December 2019, though, again, trade tensions with China contributed to a shaky economic outlook after an announcement by Trump that the trade war could go on.[25] Later that month, Democrats unveiled articles of impeachment against Trump but also passed a new trade agreement with Mexico and Canada called USMCA.

Politics, indeed, has its share of oddities.

Remember for a moment some of the primary platforms Trump ran on when he won election in 2016. Stricter trade policies, economic improvement, stock market gains, and additional jobs were all part of the message that resonated enough to win key battleground states.

Generally, those are all issues that carry more significance with investors than partisan political theater. As much as some liberals wanted to deny any positivity in the slogan, "Make America Great Again" would be framed successfully by the Trump campaign as a hopeful message.

What I tell people whenever they relay concerns about something happening in Washington is to examine fundamental principles and how they relate to any foundational effects on the economy.

Frankly, when the impeachment proceedings got rolling, the market crushed it. Trade disputes, particularly with China, and interest-rate policy imposed by the Federal Reserve still presented primary economic

---

[24] Ibid.

[25] Michael Wursthorn & Anna Isaac. *The Wall Street Journal.* December 3, 2019. "U.S. Stocks Slide After Trump Signals Further Delays to China Deal." https://www.wsj.com/articles/global-stocks-post-tepid-gains-as-investors-dismiss-tariff-threats-11575368125

concerns as the investigation launched by the Democrat-controlled House of Representatives unfolded for the world to watch.

Markets, even when they reel from various factors and experience declines, find ways to adapt.

Management teams within a large majority of American companies often adjust, too, and show strong resilience. The entrepreneurial spirit in this country is something we should never dismiss. As someone who independently started my own small business, Murray Financial Group, I know this to be true.

Many great business owners are to be applauded for accepting substantial risks and overcoming unintended faults. They took a chance, sometimes with every last bit of their savings, to build businesses that are both aspirational and profitable. This applies to all levels of business—big, medium, and small.

In Frederick, I constantly marvel at the works of the radio station, WFMD-AM, and its sister station, WFRE-FM. When it first aired in 1936, the AM station was a family-owned operation that essentially started from scratch. Several ownership groups have now implemented changes, yet WFMD and WFRE remain beacons of the community through public service.

Fundraisers are especially important to the stations, which raise a considerable amount of money for St. Jude Children's Research Hospital, as well as contributing to other charitable efforts by connecting the Frederick community with its radio and internet reach.

Bob Miller, who I banter with during my business updates each weekday morning, helps raise funds for the Salvation Army each holiday season with a program entitled "Christmas Cash for Kids." In 2020, the names of more than 1,800 kids and their parents got placed on a list. The push "The Morning Mayor" provides on the air helps raise more than $128,000 each year for that specific project, which makes Christmas much more joyful for many Frederick County families.

It's worthwhile to remember the family that started WFMD so many years ago and the legacy created over the years that continues to benefit our community. That's the kind of American entrepreneurial spirit everyone should applaud.

Events Do Matter

I don't want to leave the wrong impression after noting that political shenanigans are often considered regular behavior inside the Beltway, and, because of that, sometimes they do not influence the economy that greatly.

What happens on both a national and world stage does matter.

For example, the 9/11 terrorist attacks could be related to a pebble thrown in the middle of a pond, though that analogy is not intended to minimize the devastating effects of that horrific plot.

The dot.com bubble had begun to implode, including the unraveling of corruption at Enron and the disreputable accounting practices uncovered at Arthur Andersen. A domino effect caused the recession to worsen. In 2003, the United States marched into Iraq to fight the War on Terror.

Eventually, corporate failures at Lehman Brothers, Washington Mutual, WorldCom, General Motors, and CIT Group surpassed the 2001 collapse of Enron as the most devastating corporate bankruptcy in history.[26]

The attention generated by the accounting scandal that was central to Enron's collapse centered on fraudulent U.S. business practices. Shareholders lost $74 billion in four years, and employees lost billions in pension benefits.[27]

---

[26] Amanda Harding. CheatSheet. Sept. 13, 2018. "The Biggest Bankruptcies in America's History Prove No One Is 'Too Big to Fail.'" https://www.cheatsheet.com/money-career/the-biggest-bankruptcies-in-americas-history-prove-no-one-is-too-big-to-fail.html/

[27] Troy Segal. Investopedia. May 29, 2019. "Enron Scandal: The Fall of a Wall Street Darling." https://www.investopedia.com/updates/enron-scandal-summary/

People began wondering whether companies worldwide were worth the values reported.

On top of that, the fear of traveling after the 9/11 attacks not only impacted airlines but also all the businesses that thrive on travel. The times seemed somewhat sullen, reserved, surreal. The result negatively impacted our gross domestic product and that of other industrialized countries.

Such times make it paramount to analyze accounts and make people aware of influences that can impact the market. That played into the letter I wrote to clients the night of September 11, 2001, though their well-being topped my list of concerns. I wanted them to know I understood if they felt worried about their physical, emotional, and financial safety.

Quarterly Updates

We want clients to know they are always welcome to make an appointment and drop by. We invite them in each quarter.

As everyone knows, three months usually fly by in a blink. If they don't feel like coming back in that soon, we understand. We send reports each quarter, attached to a letter that provides an overview of economic indicators, which analyzes both domestic and international markets.

Something in that correspondence occasionally prompts clients to call, but everyone is different. Some clients will visit us each quarter, and that's great. Others rarely make a peep.

The great thing about doing radio, though, is clients feel as if they stay in touch just from listening in. Some clients will remind me of interviews or, even more often, something in the news I offered my take on. They listen in, even when they live outside the area, and tune in on the internet to the WFMD website or through the app.

When the airing for my Saturday show changed to two slots in the fall of 2019, a husband and wife (ninety-one and eighty-three) became the first to ask if I did radio anymore. When I told them the show aired at different times on Saturdays and was also podcast on iTunes, the woman grew concerned that the content varied.

Nope, I assured them. It was the same show. Ratings, in fact, have been solid over the years, a nice reflection on the format and the variety offered by bringing on guests from different financial sectors.

Building a clientele among several who tune into the show has been great for Murray Financial Group.

What's far more important to me, however, is the desire to keep relationships intact with those clients and do everything possible to grow their wealth and help them follow an efficient and effective retirement plan we continually build.

Their experiences help shape some of the opinions I have about the effects of government bureaucracy and why, from time to time, I rail on overspending and, in particular, inefficient spending.

In the case of one client in her mid-fifties, the wheezy Washington hamster wheel caused her to get out so she could maintain her sanity.

She worked for the Department of Energy and told me, quite bluntly, "I can't be around these people anymore. There's nobody who wants to work. There's no work ethic. No demand that workers pick up the pace. None of that."

The feeble malaise that seemed to shackle each and every project caused my client to get out. The job dragged her down so much she felt as if she had become a different person. For her, and I suppose many others, the Washington rat race became more of a rat nest.

Of course, then there are folks who worked in the government that joined the private side as contractors. Contracts typically are limited to three years, so there can be some lulls, but many make great money and provide insightful contributions to projects based on their experiences.

What all this reflects is even when someone is in the same general line of work with the federal government, much can vary, beginning with the level of satisfaction in the job itself.

Again, it's why one of the favorites aspects I enjoy with my job as a financial planner is getting to know my clients and figuring out the best path related to their investment and retirement needs.

Folding in Some Solutions

A favorite exercise of mine that helps people understand the importance of planning, and the need to update a retirement plan because changes are bound to happen in life, is contained to a single piece of paper. On it are a bunch of scattered numbers from one to ninety arranged randomly. I often hand this paper to clients and ask that they circle as many numbers in order as they can in sixty seconds. Of course, they bounce all around the paper, looking for one, two, three, etc.

After that, I take a copy of the same sheet of numbers and fold the paper neatly into four identical squares. One number in each square corresponds to the sequencing of four numbers. Quite often, clients who participate in this exercise often identify as many as three times as many numbers while still counting from one to ninety.

When people complete this drill, I emphasize that the difference between a scrambled mess of numbers on a full sheet of paper, and the folded assortment presented in quarter sections can be equated to the difference between having a retirement plan and flying by the seat of your pants.

1 61 41 13 42 74 14
17 9 81 70 18 22 46
45 86 34 2 30
89 21 38
49 78 50
5 69 6 90
37 85 29 82 26 10
25 33 65
53 57 54 58
73 77 66 62
79 39 32 76 16
15 71 8 40
31 3 80 24
47 83 55 56
28
7 27 52 4
51 11 67 72 12 88 60
75 48
19 23 36 20
87 43 64
35 59 63 68 44 84

Chapter Seven

Passing the Torch

G oing back to the very first meeting I have with prospective clients, one question is fundamental to the process of crafting a retirement plan for them to follow.

I ask if they have wills, trusts, and powers of attorneys in place.

This is a service I cannot perform. I do not offer legal advice, but I can point them to qualified attorneys who specialize in estate planning and elder care. Every part of someone's estate is affected by financial matters, so it only makes sense that legal directives have been drawn to protect assets and build legacy plans that incorporate their final wishes.

To stress this point, I emphasize that prospective clients should be applauded for taking a critical step to consult an experienced advisor who can examine their financial situation. This is a victory in and of itself.

So, why not plan to button up everything from a legal standpoint? Affirm that legal directives are in place or agree to meet with an attorney if a legal instrument must be drawn up or if changes are needed to an existing directive.

Even if I do not become someone's financial advisor, this pertinent dialogue could be the most important suggestion I can provide someone during our initial meeting.

"Look," I tell them, "you are taking all the time and energy to meet with a financial advisor. You are spending money to put a financial plan in place for either investing or for retirement.

"You are doing all these homework projects to find documents, verify accounts, estimate budgets, and articulate retirement ambitions. At this point, consulting with an estate attorney only makes sense."

Any dialogue about finances should include the expertise provided by an estate attorney, and for that matter an accountant. Inclusion of these professionals in crafting a retirement plan is considered sound risk management.

Those who visit with me cannot predict when their final hour will come. We must concede, however, that we're all mortal.

In addition to the desires we hope to fulfill in retirement, we must stipulate our final wishes and incorporate them into legal directives. I can even provide additional information about assets, net worth, or other financial matters if an estate attorney needs information. I'll be glad to work with whomever you decide to retain.

Frankly, I would be doing you a disservice if I did not explain how I work in conjunction with an estate attorney and, for that matter, an accountant, to create a holistic financial strategy. If I weren't to explain the need to incorporate others into the planning process, I'm not sure how we would arrive at an effective plan.

Building Trust

Introductions are the greatest tribute to any business, including that of a financial planner like myself.

It's the highest compliment we receive at Murray Financial, above and beyond someone expressing their appreciation for what you're doing or even saying thank you, though we never dismiss any niceties.

Introductions mean you earned the trust of someone who depends on you to plan what is best for life savings they worked hard to accrue and just as hard to grow.

Clients appreciate that you're honest and you have integrity. If a client volunteers an introduction, they know you're not going to make them look bad, and you're going to treat new clients the exact same way you treat all clients.

One really cool aspect is when children of clients agree to let me manage assets or help them plan for retirement. Sometimes this happens at a difficult time following the death of a parent, when assets are passed down through legal documents prepared by an estate attorney I quite possibly recommended. Over the years, I heard stories about the same kids when their parents consulted with me about retirement planning.

I remember visiting a client, Monica, just before Christmas after her husband, Stan, passed away. Their adult children sat beside her, and the family dog sat contently on Monica's lap when she remembered something I said during the planning process.

All of them smiled and commented on how Monica spoke of their inheritance, their father's wishes, and the wisdom behind seeking a professional who could help them grow those assets.

Granted, these introductions are cost-effective. The price attached is practically nothing. Yet, the feeling is also priceless knowing you will work hard to build a long, successful relationship that's mutually beneficial—sometimes for generations of family members.

Engage with Young Adults About Retirement

Doing radio for twenty-plus years as 'Your Financial Editor' certainly has enhanced my name recognition and has worked great as a marketing funnel for Murray Financial Group.

The opportunity to enlighten listeners about financial matters in the extended, hour-long format developed for the weekend show enables me to expand on fresh financial developments that happened earlier in the week.

In addition, I delve into retirement issues I address in this book and also welcome guests capable of drilling down to specifics on various topics.

Financial literacy is a concern for America.

I doubt that many millennials, and definitely not the Gen Z generation, tuned into the radio or accessed my shows off podcasts. An older demographic of retirees and pre-retirees typically composes most of the audience.

One hope I have, however, and something I encourage clients who are parents or grandparents, is to have regular discussions with young adults, teens, and even kids about the importance of saving.

If they're young, their diligence can help them purchase something they dearly want. Or, they can watch their savings grow and perhaps learn to place money into a certificate of deposit or purchase a share or two of stock.

Once you get them into grade school, and perhaps even earlier, they're not too young to get into the habit of saving money and learning how the value of that money can grow through different vehicles with different levels of risk.

Not long after our sons, Devin and Garrett, left our house, each of them began contributing at least 10 percent of their pay into retirement accounts. I was proud of them, especially since I assured them that, once they began saving, they wouldn't miss the money. Out of sight, out of mind, essentially.

The sooner anyone gets started saving, particularly for retirement, the more an account can grow over time. If you're to save two hundred dollars a month (a bit less than fifty dollars per week) for thirty-five years, your money will grow to the following amounts based on different interest rates:

- 3 percent: $148,680

- 6 percent: $286,370

- 12 percent: $1.3 million

Show those totals sometime to a young adult venturing into the real world of full-time work. They may feel as if they're overwhelmed by rent or a mortgage, utilities, student loans, a car loan, and other expenses, especially when attempting to make ends meet.

Chances are, however, that young adults might discover a spare fifty dollars a week by being a little choosier on how often they order their favorite latte, craft beer, or sushi combination. Also, they can go find a used late-model vehicle that gets them around just fine and doesn't cost near as much to finance.

Again, if they get in the habit of saving through an automatic withdrawal, they'll likely forget about that sliver of their paycheck going into a 401(k) or some other retirement account. This is particularly true with direct deposit, since pay stubs aren't generated on paper and finding that information requires online investigation.

An additional point I stress for younger adults, and for that matter anyone forty-five or younger, is not to plan on full coverage for Social Security, Social Security Disability, Medicare, and Medicaid.

At some point, the legislative and executive branches of our federal government must come to grips with this country's debt load and the problems posed by entitlement programs. Changes will likely result in cutbacks in distributions, making it even more imperative to save for retirement.

Wealth Is Not a Bad Word

A negative overtone is often attached to wealthy Americans. At least one candidate in the presidential races of 2016 and 2020, Bernie Sanders, advocated "there should be no billionaires. We are going to tax their extreme wealth."[28]

As much as wealthy people are made out to be plutocrats, robber barons, or fat cats, it's every bit as true that many contribute immensely to American society and culture.

One of my personal favorites is John Pierpont Morgan, who moved to New York in 1858 and became one of the giants in the Industrial Revolution. His role in reorganizing railroads, merging companies to form General Electric, and creation of the first billion-dollar corporation, U.S. Steel, are just some of his contributions to business.

Although he is often depicted as a greedy financier, Morgan helped avert a financial panic in 1907 with his own assets, and those he convinced fellow businessmen to contribute.

His detailed eye for the fine arts and generous donations drove him to augment the collection at the Metropolitan Museum of Art into one of the world's finest. He also became a trustee for the American Museum of Natural History.

Christopher Levenick reported these traits in a short biography he wrote about Morgan for *Philanthropy*, a quarterly magazine published by The Philanthropic Roundtable, which lists Morgan as a member of its hall of fame.

Levenick wrote that fierce devotion to the Episcopal faith prompted Morgan to meet for three-week intervals with bishops every three years for theological discussions. Morgan served on a committee that revised the *Book of Common Prayer*, which Morgan committed to memory,

---

[28] Chris Cillizza. cnn.com. September 24, 2019. "Bernie Sanders wants to get rid of billionaires. All of them." https://www.cnn.com/2019/09/24/politics/bernie-sanders-ultra-wealth-tax-billionaires/index.html

according to biographer Jean Strouse. That feat is certainly believable considering Morgan could fluently speak French and German, while also being considered a gifted mathematician.

When Morgan died in 1913, newspaper accounts estimated the value of his estate to be $80 million, a sizeable sum, though not as substantial as other wealthy businessmen of his time. His commitment to both finance and philanthropy seemed intertwined.[29]

The last will and testament of J.P. Morgan exceeded 10,000 words and included thirty-seven articles. I consider a quote he placed into the very first article, which conveys the everlasting value of faith, to be a vital message I wish to share in closing this book.

"I commit my soul into the hands of my Savior, in full confidence that, having redeemed it and washed it in His most precious blood, He will present it faultless before my heavenly Father; and I entreat my children to maintain and defend, at all hazard and at any cost of personal sacrifice, the blessed doctrine of the complete atonement for sin through the blood of Jesus Christ, once offered, and through that alone."

---

[29] Christopher Levenick. philanthropyroundtable.org. 2019. "J.P. Morgan." https://www.philanthropyroundtable.org/almanac/people/hall-of-fame/detail/j.-p.-morgan

The 2020 Coronavirus

Toward the end of the period in which I wrote this book, the coronavirus outbreak hit the United States in March 2020. The virus also became known as COVID-19 because it surfaced in 2019 after being found to be genetically related to the coronavirus responsible for the SARS outbreak of 2003.[30]

During my time advising Murray Financial Group clients, the market fallout resulting from COVID-19 marked the third big market tumble, joining the dot.com crash of 2000 that preceded a second fallout from the 2001 terrorist attacks and the 2008 crash tied to the housing sector.

The coronavirus erupted quickly and not only proved to be a domestic disruption but also an international crisis. The shutdown of businesses and imposition of stay-at-home directives marked an unprecedented period for Americans. The death toll from COVID-19 has at the time of publishing, exceed 200,000, while unemployment

---

[30] World Health Organization. 2020. "Naming the coronavirus disease (COVID-19) and the virus that causes it." https://www.who.int/emergencies/diseases/novel-coronavirus-2019/technical-guidance/naming-the-coronavirus-disease-(covid-2019)-and-the-virus-that-causes-it#:~:text=The%20International%20Committee%20on%20Taxonomy,SARS%20outbreak%20of%202003

claims exceed 40 million.[31] A market that had set records for bull expansion, including an S&P 500 record of 3,386 on February 19, 2020, quickly plummeted into bear status on March 12.[32]

For the week ending March 21, 2020, a record-breaking 3.3 million Americans applied for unemployment benefits as the nation's economy essentially shut down. Individuals filing for unemployment benefits that week topped the previous weekly record by nearly five-fold.[33]

In April 2020, unemployment reached 14.4 percent before dropping to 13 percent in May. The turn of events proved startling, however, after the country logged one of its lowest monthly unemployment rates on record—3.8 percent in February.[34]

The effects of market whiplash had been felt during that short stretch, too. Following the downturn, a rapid surge provided the economy a quick bounce. By the beginning of June 2020, a significant portion of market losses had already been recovered.[35]

The blessing in all this for Murray Financial Group proved to be the fortitude of our clients.

Although the effects of the coronavirus seemed unreal, especially when compounded by the effects of senseless rioting and looting stemming from an unfortunate police incident in Minnesota, our clients

[31] Kelly Anne Smith. Forbes.com. June 2, 2020. "Stock Markets Are Surging. Is This A Bear Market Rally?" https://www.forbes.com/advisor/investing/bear-market-rally/
[32] Fred Imbert. CNBC.com. March 21, 2020. "Stocks can return to records early next year if the US can curb coronavirus spread, says JPMorgan." https://www.cnbc.com/2020/03/21/stocks-can-return-to-records-early-next-year-if-the-us-can-curb-coronavirus-spread-says-jpmorgan.html
[33] Heidi Chung. Yahoo.com. March 26, 2020. "U.S. jobless claims skyrocket to 3.283 million." https://finance.yahoo.com/news/coronavirus-weekly-initial-unemployment-claims-march-21-153036254.html
[34] Rakesh Kochhar. pewresearch.org. June 11, 2020. "Unemployment rose higher in three months of COVID-19 than it did in two years of the Great Recession." https://www.pewresearch.org/fact-tank/2020/06/11/unemployment-rose-higher-in-three-months-of-covid-19-than-it-did-in-two-years-of-the-great-recession/
[35] Kelly Anne Smith. Forbes.com. June 2, 2020. "Stock Markets Are Surging. Is This A Bear Market Rally?" https://www.forbes.com/advisor/investing/bear-market-rally/

rode out the waves of discord. Nobody ran for the hills looking to live off deer meat, a stringer of fish, or wild berries. Our firm lost no assets under management.

Yes, COVID-19 and the new normal it created left a scary path in its wake. We all adapted to new ways of doing business and, frankly, a new way of life. I like to look at the good that came out of it, especially for those who felt a refreshed sense of purpose and a renewed set of values based on faith, family, and friendships.

Much like I did after 9/11 with the letter I sent to clients following those horrific acts of war on our country, I organized my thoughts and collected data.

I then sent emails to clients as weekly updates to inform them of the characteristics inherent to the coronavirus outbreak, the severe market fluctuations it caused, and the adaptations it manifested. I attempted to calm any fears and cautioned clients not to get too frightened about the events unfolding.

The robust condition of the American economy going into the negative impact of the coronavirus is a point I emphasized because the strength it previously exhibited would boost any recovery.

My habit is to always look for the silver lining. I enjoy projecting that kind of spirit and attitude on my radio appearances and in meetings with clients because, well, that's who I am. Life's good.

So, in the emails I sent to clients, I attempted to reinforce certain procedures inherent in a response to any market downturn, including the rebalancing of portfolios to rotate out of certain classes and exposure. Clients appreciate it when you inform them of such measures, but moreover, it's the right thing to do.

During periods of financial uncertainty and market turbulence, they need to know someone is there for them, and I'm happy to handle that obligation as an independent fiduciary who isn't shackled by constraints imposed at the big box firms.

Of course, everyone's a little different and so, too, are the characteristics in their portfolios and the goals they desire in retirement.

When unemployment rose as one of the issues stemming from COVID-19, I remember sharing on my radio program a common question among consumers: "What's the right amount of cash to keep on the sidelines?" I went on to say, the answer is both simple and complex: "It's different for everyone."

A customary industry response is to stipulate a person builds an emergency fund that meets three to six months of expenses. That's a starting point if you're laid off, get furloughed for an indefinite period, or have an emergency arise.

But really, it takes more thought than just a simple accounting exercise to ascertain how much you might need. Some people like to have a lot of cash sitting around, and they're fine with that rather than having a broker telling them to invest that bundle so it can potentially grow.

Not everyone is wired that way, however. The coronavirus outbreak reflected that mindset within those who feel better knowing they have their "security blanket" of cash set aside when the markets get choppy. It's something I make sure to discuss with clients as part of our planning strategies by asking questions like:

- "What will make you comfortable when the market goes through a correction?"
- "How much dry powder do you want to set aside?"

This consideration can be especially important for retirees because, if they're withdrawing funds from retirement accounts and did so in March 2020, they actually sold at a substantial loss.

So, if you can turn off that spigot and avoid taking money out of investment accounts, taking the money out of a money market account instead, you know those funds are liquid and haven't been affected by a market downturn.

Additional silver linings could spring from the pandemic. For example, in America, it's important people finally realize certain characteristics about our supply chains and precisely what can happen if we don't exert enough control over them.

Foreign ownership of meat processing plants, where COVID-19 infections spread terribly in some states, deserves to be scrutinized. Included among those processors is Smithfield Foods, which shut down three plants because of abundant coronavirus cases. Smithfield Foods happens to be owned by a Chinese billionaire.[36]

It's important to take a long, hard look at some of the suppliers in this country and consider different approaches for our supply chains. If food isn't a national security issue, I don't know what is.

On the medical front, the outbreak could inspire advances for producing vaccines, medications, treatment, and therapy, especially after breakneck work commenced shortly after the outbreak. Those health initiatives could stretch much further than just treatments developed for COVID-19.[37]

An element that could have a considerable impact on retirement planning will be the future of long-term care facilities. Outbreaks at some of those centers could trigger changes in that industry. Who knows? It could become more common for sons and daughters to bring elderly parents into their homes, much like some Asian cultures.[38]

Bringing COVID-19 to a personal level, Carole and I have always maintained close relationships with those we love, and, again, I think the coronavirus reinforced our family ties and values.

---

[36] Jennifer Wang. April 16, 2020. Forbes. "The Chinese Billionaire Whose Company Owns Troubled Pork Processor Smithfield Foods." https://www.forbes.com/sites/jenniferwang/2020/04/16/the-chinese-billionaire-whose-company-owns-troubled-pork-processor-smithfield-foods/#4c94fc62c55d

[37] Nicoletta Lanese. Livescience.com. April 16, 2020. "When will a COVID-19 vaccine be ready?" https://www.livescience.com/coronavirus-covid-19-vaccine-timeline.html

[38] Richard Hartung. todayonline.com. Dec. 15, 2019. "Children taking care of parents' needs: Changing norms and what to expect." https://www.todayonline.com/singapore/children-taking-care-parents-needs-changing-norms-and-what-expect

Our oldest son, Devin, had just relocated in West Palm Beach, Florida, one of the regions hardest hit by the coronavirus. He continued to travel in his marketing position, and we're thankful he's healthy, energetic, and determined to do well as he embarks on his career.

Our other son, Garrett, had just traveled to Asia for advanced training as a Marine. After getting chosen for that training, he couldn't do much of anything. We could sense his frustrations, but he realized the safety precautions taken at his base were appropriate.

Our daughter, Morgan, missed out on a couple of the spring activities eagerly anticipated by a high school senior: baccalaureate and commencement. The seniors at Glenelg traditionally head for the beach, and Morgan's class got to do so after some rescheduling. Morgan accepted all the unusual circumstances and pushed right through it.

Across America, COVID-19 certainly impacted many lives, not only because of the financial fallout but also because families could not visit loved ones because of hospital visitation bans. Of course, we all feel for those we lost to the virus, too.

Throughout the beginning of the whole ordeal I could not help but think about pundits and politicians so desperate to turn the tables that they actually spoke of wanting a recession in this country. To some extent, they got their wish.

But let's look at precisely what that wrought—increased unemployment and suicide rates, mortgage foreclosures and food lines, school closures, and manufacturing cutbacks.

The airline and hospitality industries got battered, leaving us to wonder what protocols might be in place when Americans begin boarding flights and dining out with any degree of regularity again. As for entertainment options, virtually anything performed on a stage or in a stadium became a no-go and adversely affected the social fabric of this country.

Those who hoped for a recession merely for political gain need to own that. No matter how much you dislike somebody, you can't wish the effects of unemployment, mental illness, or hunger on anyone.

It makes me glad to look for a silver lining anywhere I can, humbled to earn the trust of clients who desire a financial professional looking out for them, and proud to have family and friends rooted in admirable values and strong faith.

4-H Showtime

P eople who are the salt of the earth naturally make life on the farm enjoyable.

In my case, my wife Carole's parents are instructors, helpers, and role models all rolled into one vibrant duo with impeccable character. When this book was written, Dave was 90 and Ann was 85. They would still wake up every day before dawn and continue to do chores on their own property after spending years running a dairy operation.

Years ago, our 4-H extension office approached Dave and Ann about helping kids gain an opportunity to show farm animals at the county fair. Many kids in Howard County are raised in homes with small acreage. The kids and their families are interested in nurturing animals, but their land is insufficient to raise large animals, particularly cattle.

Even though these kids are interested in farming, perhaps raising chickens or rabbits at their home, the opportunity to show large livestock at the county fair never materializes.

As with virtually anything in the agricultural industry, when Dave and Ann considered the 4-H request to join in the lease program, the conversation eventually turned to pricing. When asked how much families would need to fork over to pay for leasing their dairy heifers,

Carole's parents never thought for one second about profiting from the venture. "How about a dollar?" Dave asked.

Dave and Ann's 4-H-ers

For years Dave and Ann involved themselves in that program, which attracts kids from settings that are typically rural in nature, though 4-H certainly welcomes people of all beliefs and backgrounds. Head, Heart, Hands, and Health represent the four Hs in 4-H and are values members embrace through various programs.

We usually have around fifteen to twenty-five dairy heifers any given year. The lease program enables kids to learn to care for the heifers and show the animals at the county fair. The show heifers are still kept on our land, but the kids come at least three days a week to work with them, depending on the time and commitment they put into the program.

Growing Up

The week of the fair is busy. Not only must the heifers be hauled for showing, but the kids must also be well-trained in aspects such as getting the animals to lead, proper showmanship, and washing and brushing the animals down. They care for the animals after learning concepts and techniques at our barn and various workshops.

Putting in the Work

Eventually the kids get to deck out in their dress whites for the formal shows at the fair, where awards and ribbons are presented.

After working as hard as they did to prepare their leased heifer for the fair, it's always a thrill to see those kids and their radiant smiles the day they get to formally show their prize heifers.

These kids come from good families with parents who recognize the effort and responsibilities involved with showing heifers as an experience their children will value for the rest of their lives.

For me, I'm mindful of that summer I accepted an invitation from a buddy to work for a dairy operation that happened to belong to my future in-laws. On occasion, I still think of the chance to meet Carole and just how lucky I have been to be with her and how fortunate I am to interact and learn from her resourceful parents.

For us personally, though, one highlight each year is right in our backyard. The 4-H kids are coming to our home to learn how to care for and show heifers then compete at the nearby county fair—the end reward for providing local youths something to do with their hands other than holding a smart phone.

It's Showtime!

Kids eat together, play together, and take part in the fair parade. They also enjoy an epic water battle at the wash rack on the last day of the fair!

Of course, the 4-H kids aren't at our barn all the time. Much of the process of caring for the heifers falls on Carole and myself.

We are careful never to call ourselves farmers or ranchers, because we're not. My occupation is obviously as a financial professional who helps clients achieve their financial goals. I just really enjoy helping kids experience agricultural opportunities on the side.

Abundant Blessings

Bob Miller, 'The Morning Mayor'

M orning radio shows can be a different beast.

For starters, you beat any and all traffic getting to work. The highways and streets are barren. So, too, is the studio when I walk in.

Yet, over the past twenty or so years doing the *Morning News Express* for WFMD-AM (930) in Frederick, the feel, the vibe, and the information we dispense has developed a natural flow. It excites me to know another new day has dawned, there's plenty of news to report and analyze, and we're around to help folks get up and going in the morning.

Some of the news, of course, comes out of the financial world. People who follow developments from Wall Street are keenly interested in much of what happens during today's twenty-four-hour news cycle. At least a bit, and sometimes a lot, of what transpires each day in the markets reflects the impact of events happening around the globe.

I don't profess to know a great deal about ups and downs of the financial sector. Perhaps one reason I don't try too hard to dive deep into different nuances regarding trades, indicators, and trends has been the presence of Chris Murray and the financial updates he provides three times each weekday morning.

By now, I can barely remember doing our station's morning routine without him. I can assure you I cringe just a little whenever he tells us he won't be available because he's leaving town for a few days or going to be busy showing dairy heifers at one of the fairs he attends.

I'm like, "Dude, you're ruining my show when you're not on because I'm horrible at pulling together the financial report." I'm just kidding around with him, but in all seriousness, I enjoy the information he provides. Chris makes me feel a bit smarter every day with what he prepares for our listeners, and I appreciate that.

I give him a break, though. I don't have him come to the office in the wee hours each morning. He calls in to do his reports after providing me a heads-up the night before about topics he will address. That helps me set up his delivery with a little banter, which is always fun.

Details Chris uncovers, along with the broad scope of topics he touches on, keep the reports fresh and provide insights listeners won't hear anywhere else.

This is particularly true of the weekend shows Chris airs. *Your Financial Editor* has drawn a wide range of guests, including many power players from the business and political arenas, given that Frederick is a bedroom community of Washington D.C.

Some big-time financial types with pretty deep pockets live in our area, and Chris runs right alongside those people with ease. He also appeals to rural folks in small Maryland communities such as Woodsboro, where I live. Chris can disseminate the same information and make it understandable, and enjoyable, for someone who dresses in jeans and work boots, those who wear tailored three-piece suits, and everyone whose fashion preference lies somewhere in between.

This is because Chris dresses just like them. I suppose he's a bit of a city slicker-slash-farm boy. He married a farm girl, Carole, then got his start as a businessman running his own landscaping company. He transitioned into financial services and now is as comfortable in a suit advising clients as he is in jeans forking out stalls for the cows.

That makes him unique, which is a nice quality to have when you're attempting to stand out among the big brokerage firms of the financial industry.

When Chris calls in for his updates, he's already been up for quite a while tending to whatever demands attention on the farmstead he calls home. Yet, he swiftly switches into business mode and is fully aware of developments in the markets and specific financial sectors.

Making anything relatable to a vast array of people is a talent.

Doing so on radio, without any prior experience behind a microphone, is even more impressive.

When Chris started out with his contributions for WFMD, the timing pretty much coincided with the start of his own independent financial practice in Frederick. Exposure on radio made sense as a way for Chris to grow his business, but after getting to know him so well for all these years, I know he also found it to be a way he could help people.

Understand Chris does not get paid a dime for his updates or his hour-long show on the weekend. Under such circumstances, many people would make sure to spend much of their time promoting their business, but Chris doesn't do that. I've told him it's fine to plug Murray Financial Group, but he's content just to come on and be informational rather than promotional.

Our station has a program called, "Christmas Cash for Kids," which we sponsor through the Salvation Army. We purchase and present gifts to kids in Frederick County and also give food baskets to their families. Each year, Chris provides a generous donation, without fanfare, that helps our charity tremendously.

The annual contribution from Chris again illustrates his humble, modest approach. I remember asking him about it once because I realized he could be capitalizing more on the promotional platform available to him as a regular on radio. He just told me, "I'm good. Being here and doing this kind of promotes me already, and that's fine."

Then I found out first-hand what Chris meant by that.

He hosts a dinner each year for his clients, and the first time I attended I saw a lot of people I know who listen to our station. Those appearances Chris makes at 5:50, 6:50, and 7:50 each weekday morning, which established the persona for *Your Financial Editor*, truly did promote his business without any on-air salesmanship from him.

Again, that's who Chris is, and it's reflected in his delivery.

WFMD is a conservative station that airs conservative programming. The tenor of our morning show blazes that path to begin each day. Chris believes in conservative principles. Listeners can certainly gather that from his updates each weekday or from the in-depth commentary and interviews with guests that fill out his weekend shows.

But he is never in your face or overt about his viewpoints. His nature coincides with his desire to help people leading up to, and through, retirement. People respect that approach, including those Chris interviews for *Your Financial Editor*.

He attracts some heavy hitters. I attended a symposium once that Chris got involved in and saw him on stage speaking to Jeffrey Lacker, the former president of the Federal Reserve Bank of Richmond.

The reaction from the media in attendance to anything Lacker said, and the impression made by someone from the Federal Reserve, really caught my attention. Here was Chris, a tag team partner off our morning show, acting as something of a moderator and prompting insightful comments that made news.

Over the years, I can tell Chris has become more comfortable asking tougher questions. Having the knowledge to be able to ask such questions and do it in a way that is informative and entertaining, symbolizes how much Chris has grown in radio.

Coming into this he had already developed his skills as a financial professional. Now, he's a radio personality.

Believe me, it's been fun hearing practically every word of it play out for my friend, Chris Murray.

Family Ties

Chris and Family

Our backyard at the first home Carole and I lived in after we married probably should have been manicured in a meticulous fashion. Artistic enough, perhaps, to be endorsed by Better Homes and Gardens. This is because my first business venture specialized in landscaping.

Yet, I laugh about the 3-acre tract we purchased and how I channeled my, uhh, "earthly instincts" and turned some of the property into a makeshift training ground for motocross racing.

My older brother Steve and I started racing together. He wanted to mentor me as someone concerned with how his kid brother might get along in high school while raised by a single parent, my mom. He knew, too, that I would probably find motocross to be a fun pursuit.

The competition led to two periods revving highly tuned bikes across abrupt hills and tight turns. Not only did I compete into my thirties, I also steered my own kids into taking on insanely tough dirt tracks.

Once our oldest son, Devin, began racing, his younger brother, Garrett, began learning the sport on a smaller bike. Our daughter, Morgan, who is our youngest child, tagged along, of course, with Carole, who was great at helping organize our family team. The Mid-Atlantic motocross circuit became a home away from home.

With my sons getting involved, I launched a second go at racing and attacked it hard enough that a nasty spill left me with a broken back. After coping with rehabilitation, I gradually regained my strength while working with a personal trainer. I raced again for a brief period after my injury but refrained from attempting even the slightest imitation of Evel Knievel.

Nonetheless, I treasured the times our family packed up and made race weekends an outing. I suppose they didn't share the sentiment whenever they wanted to sleep through their morning alarm. However, all three learned to pitch in. Each showed dairy heifers at the county and state fairs, just like kids from the community who participated in the dairy leasing program to gain the experience, and enjoyment, from preparing and showing farm animals.

Our own kids also raised and showed pigs. Devin bought a Camaro off the money he earned from livestock sales. Garrett began saving for a pickup from his earnings. Morgan became involved, too, and showed both heifers and pigs through her senior year in high school, which was her final year in 4-H.

Each of our children has been active in activities and sports at Glenelg, the same high school Carole and I attended. Devin played lacrosse, Garrett wrestled as a four-year varsity starter, and Morgan played field hockey. (Fun fact: The Glenelg High School yearbook is fittingly called *The Palindrome*.)

As this is being written, Morgan is a freshman in college, pursuing a degree in educational special needs. This passion began when she was in middle school, when she began assisting special needs students. A girl she befriended found it difficult to communicate, yet she trusted Morgan, who would hold the girl's hand and accompany her to classes.

Morgan Playing Field Hockey

A similar connection between Morgan and other students soon developed. High school teachers noticed the way Morgan bonded with others and allowed her to become a peer tutor a year before most students are accepted into the program. The kindness Morgan demonstrates and her willingness to help others is truly a gift.

Our son, Garrett, is in the Marine Corps, stationed in the 1st Battalion, 6th Marines (1/6) at Camp Lejeune in North Carolina where he is preparing for advanced infantry school after returning from his deployment in Asia. We consider ourselves a patriotic family and wholeheartedly support Garrett's enlistment. He joined the Marines after we encouraged Garrett to attend college for one year, just to follow through on the exemplary grades he achieved in high school.

After that first year of college, Garrett came into my office at home and said virtually the same thing he told us after graduating from Glenelg. He still wanted to be a Marine. "Well, you did what we asked you to do," I told him. "You went to school, and I couldn't be more proud of you—that you want to join the Marines and serve our country. So, go ahead and get after it."

Garrett Winning a Wrestling Match

Devin is a graduate of James Madison University, where he earned a degree in business marketing. He participated in the ROTC and trained with the Army at Fort Knox. A medical issue, which required surgery on an infected arm, kept him from gaining a six-month certification update needed to be in the ROTC. That circumstance caused Devin to change his degree path after leaving an international business curriculum and the ROTC.

Through my business background, I can certainly detect Devin's strong appetite for business education and willingness to learn all about his profession and excel at his job. His first position out of college enabled him to join an international company, TTI, which is based in Hong Kong and has an office in West Palm Beach, Florida.

Helping Devin make the move was still trying for Carole and I, even though Garrett left the house first to join the Marines. A hurricane just happened to be ravaging Florida the day Devin had first been scheduled to fly down there. He quickly was promoted to manager, however, and relocated to Charlotte, North Carolina, where he oversees a team of twelve.

Devin Playing Lacrosse for JMU

I can affirm with great pleasure and satisfaction that Carole and I are blessed to have such wonderful children—young adults, actually—who are mature beyond their years and motivated to help others.

Acknowledgments

To the many family members and friends who have provided incredible guidance, assistance, and support throughout my life and my career. Words cannot express how fortunate I feel each day to be surrounded by faithful, caring people.

The creation of Murray Financial Group, my own "sandbox" in the financial industry, fulfilled my desire to become a local, independent, fiduciary. That role has enabled me to build longstanding personal relationships with wonderful people I can call loyal clients.

I would be remiss not to mention the assistance I have received providing the level of service that clients of Murray Financial Group deserve. Many faithful workers have helped with our endeavors since we opened in 1995.

Christopher Murray

C hris got his start in the industry in 1989, and, after working for other financial companies, he decided to follow his drive to help others. In 1995, he founded Murray Financial Group, a firm dedicated to helping individuals and families overcome the challenges of creating a steady financial foundation. He loves working hand-in-hand with his clients to understand their financial goals and help them build a clear path to achieving them.

Chris has passed the Series 65 securities exam and holds life and health insurance licenses in Maryland and other states.

He was recognized nine times as best financial planner by *Frederick Magazine* and hosts the popular radio show *Your Financial Editor*. Chris also provides live business updates Monday through Friday at 5:50 a.m., 6:50 a.m., and 7:50 a.m. on 930 WFMD-AM.

In his free time, Chris enjoys spending time with friends and family.

"Best Of" is an annual survey conducted by Frederick Magazine. The winner is chosen by an online vote of the general public and no specific criteria is used to determine the winner. The majority of voters may not be clients of Murray Financial, Inc. The designation is not representative of any one client's experience and is not indicative of future performance.